THE WAY FORWARD FOR LEGAL EDUCATION ⇢

The Way Forward *for*

Carolina Academic Press · Durham, North Carolina

Legal Education

DAVID I. C. THOMSON

Professor of Practice and
John C. Dwan Professor of Online Learning
University of Denver, Sturm College of Law

Library of Congress cataloging-in-publication data is available at catalog.loc.gov

LCCN 2022051422
ISBN 978-1-5310-2396-6
eISBN 978-1-5310-2397-3

Carolina Academic Press
700 Kent Street
Durham, North Carolina 27701
(919) 489-7486
www.cap-press.com

Printed in the United States of America

For Kathy

and

for Fred

Contents

Introduction

Two decades into the twenty-first century, it now seems likely that among the most influential developments of the century will be the increasing ubiquity of technology, and in particular the democratization of information access and creation through the delivery system of the Internet. This influence is already far-reaching—from the crowd sourcing of a vast encyclopedia to the democratization of information using a system of messaging limited to 280 characters at a time. And on the negative side, it has allowed the manipulation of what is reliable news, and this has had significant consequences as well, including the undermining of our democratic institutions. Not long ago, we were mostly content consumers, while now an unprecedented number of us are content creators as well. The impact of these changes will only increase and be felt well into the future. In many ways, the impact of this seismic shift in communication will define our future.

We are now coming to understand that the educational system we have today was created at a time when information was scarce. But information is no longer scarce, and that simple difference will have a profound impact on the educational system we will have in this century, and—in many ways—it already has. The question for this book is, what changes can we implement that will position legal education as we know it for a new educational paradigm that remains to be determined?

Technological fear and resistance has always been with us. Socrates was suspicious of books, fearing that they would become a substitute for wisdom, and teachers of the late nineteenth century railed against the evil of blackboards, fearing that students would not focus on the lecturer if he turned his back on them. We consider these examples of technological resistance foolish today. Allan Kay wisely said: "Technology is anything that wasn't around when you were born."[1] In other words, the car was technology to your great-grandfather, but to us, it seems commonplace. Further, it is hard—if not impossible—to foresee the full impact of a new technology when the prototype is in front of us. Few understood what the invention of the telephone would allow, and who would even want one, and for what purpose. The CEO of Digital Equipment Corporation laughed when presented with the PC, famously commenting: "There is no reason for any individual to have a computer in his home."[2]

Because of fear, resistance, and inability to understand future impact of new technology, we often react to it in a binary fashion. We believe that the new thing will completely replace the old, and we fear that. We fear it because there are good things about the old way of doing things, and we fear losing those. But the history of technology tells us that rarely does the new technology completely replace the old. While we have many fewer landline telephones, we still have many of them, even while we have hundreds of millions of cellphones. Well before the Kindle—which merely made them easier to purchase and read—we had electronic books, and yet we still have millions of print books being printed and read in that form today. There was so much hand-wringing that bookstores would all die.[3] They have not died.[4] There are numerous other examples, but what is important is that we let go of thinking that the embrace of the new always comes with the death of the old. More common is a hybridization of the two, or in some cases, simple co-existence, interplay, and mutual growth.

In 2020, we learned some of these lessons in education through the impact of COVID-19 related shutdowns. Fortunately, we all had computers in our homes, and internet access, and we were able to adjust, and rapidly. Was it

---

1. Paul Ashcroft & Garrick Jones, Digital Humans: Thriving in an Online World 8 (Wiley 2022).

2. Christopher Cerf & Victor Navasky, The Experts Speak: The Definitive Compendium of Authoritative Misinformation 209, 338 (Pantheon 1984).

3. Lev Grossman, *The Death of the Bookstore was Greatly Exaggerated*, Time, June 30, 2022, at 54–55.

4. Mike Peed, *Booksellers Fight Back as 5 New Stores Open*, NY Sun (January 15, 2007) https://www.nysun.com/article/arts-booksellers-fight-back-as-5-new-stores-open; *see also* Lewis Buzbee, *Back on Main Street: A Writer Takes Comfort in Independent Bookstores, Which Seem to be Rebounding*, 102 Phi Kappa Phi Forum 20, 20–21 (2022).

perfect? Of course not. We have much yet to learn about how to facilitate deep and optimized learning at a distance.

In education—when a student learns something—that event happens through the interplay of knowledge, guidance, and coaching. When these connections take place, it is a moment of alchemy. Universities facilitate thousands of these moments every day. Indeed, this is one of the reasons most teachers work in educational settings and do the work they do: because of the alchemistic nature of these moments they are hard to pin down, describe, and put in a box. It is like trying to describe what makes something funny. We must be wary of purported precision in our work. The many moments of alchemy that happen in educational settings are precious, and space for them must be preserved.

But to think that seriously engaging with methodologies for hybrid and online learning will by definition destroy those precious moments is both short-sighted and not supported by the history of technology. Indeed, such a position has been widely disproven in the maelstrom of the Covid pandemic (although admittedly not perfectly for all students all the time). And so the interesting conversation is how to nurture—and even strengthen—these moments of connection, surprise, and knowing while simultaneously looking for ways to make more of them possible in a new world, and work out the few bugs that remain. This requires deep engagement and experimentation. Without that, we will be lost. The option to do nothing is still an option, but it is becoming increasingly clear what the result of that choice would be—stagnation and unbearable cost pressure. There may be strategies available to run out the string a little bit longer, but the ultimate result of doing nothing is not in question, and it is not good.

We have some time, probably more than we think. There is always a "Chicken Little" aspect to these discussions, particularly from vendors and evangelists. But the change we are wrestling with will not happen overnight; it will be gradual. It took forty years for the zipper to move most clothing construction away from button fasteners.[5] On that scale, we are only half-way through this transition. But the course we set now will be determinative of the place we end up.

At the same time, a two-pronged reckoning is coming to legal education, and we must address both sides more urgently. First is that our democratic

5. Robert Friedel, Zipper: An Exploration in Novelty, 13, 123 (W.W. Norton and Company 1994).

institutions are under attack. There are those who believe that if the "system" will not change the way they want, they must burn it down.[6] We have learned throughout the world in the last century (in particular) that an autocracy is the inevitable result of the breakdown of democracy, and in an autocracy, there is much reduced need for lawyers, and law schools. We must take this threat more seriously than we have and build up the legitimacy of the law school enterprise to help insulate it—and our democracy and the rule of law—from further attack. Second is the long-overdue broadening of our understanding of systemic racism and legal education's role in perpetuating it. It is a fact that the vaunted halls of law school—for most of its 130-year history—have been closed to all but a comparative trickle of students who are members of historically underrepresented groups. We underserve the society of the future if this continues. Instead, we can strengthen the legitimacy and extend the proper purpose of legal education if we address systemic racism embedded in the structure of law schools boldly and forthrightly. Some dramatic changes must be made to address these issues—slow change will not fix them.

So not only *how* we educate, but *who* we educate in law schools must change.

Like all authors, I can only offer this book from the perspective of someone with my particular background in the law and legal education. I practiced law for twenty years—mostly litigation in a large New York firm, and at the Department of Justice as a trial attorney—before switching to full-time teaching nineteen years ago. During my practice, I served as an adjunct professor at two schools for seven years, so I have taught in a law school setting for twenty-six years total, the first time being thirty-eight years ago. Although I have taught Administrative Law and Civil Discovery Law, my primary teaching load is to teach the first year Lawyering Process course. I have written and presented about law school pedagogy and teaching with technology for most of the last nineteen years, throughout the U.S., and in China, Moscow, Canada, Japan, the U.K., Australia, and the Czech Republic.

This book offers a vision for the near future of legal education. It is, in some ways, a "follow up" or a "follow on" book to my previous book about legal education, *Law School 2.0—Legal Education for a Digital Age*. That book—written

6. Ronald Radosh, *Steve Bannon, Trump's Top Guy, Told Me He Was 'a Leninist*, Daily Beast (Aug. 22, 2016), https://www.thedailybeast.com/steve-bannon-trumps-top-guy-told-me-he-was-a-leninist.

a year before the financial "Econolypse" of 2009 and eleven years before the Covid pandemic—predicted many of the forces that converged on legal education after its publication. This one seeks to do the same—and to describe, as that one attempted to do, our best path forward.

David Thomson
Denver, Colorado
November 1, 2022

Dedication

This book is dedicated to Federico (Fred) Cheever, my colleague on the Denver Law faculty, and friend. Fred, a dedicated environmental lawyer and teacher, died—in June 2017 at the age of 60—too young, doing something he loved: river rafting on the Green River in Northwest Colorado with his family. It was a tragedy, but one of those tragedies that is deeply multi-layered, like the geological strata of the surrounding Rocky Mountains. He death was, of course, a terrible loss to his wife Mary, whom he loved immensely and for whom he hung the moon. And also a terrible loss to his two daughters, Elizabeth and Laurel, whom he loved with a particular intensity—one we both shared that was borne by our emotional suffering as children and our determination to break the cycle with our own. Both of his daughters were just emerging into an adulthood in full flower, but still benefiting from the love and steady advice of their father.

A terrible loss to the faculty at Denver Law. Every faculty—whether in law or not—has one Switzerland, one member with modest gravitas who can see the sometimes contentious issues from both sides and articulate a through path that respects all concerned. Fred was that faculty member for us. A terrible loss for his many colleagues, both at the law school and not, who admired him and his work at the university level in the Faculty Senate, and in establishing the Sustainability Council and many other such initiatives over his more than two decades of service to the university. Fred was that kind of selfless giver of his time to university initiatives that he was, at times, taken advantage of—about which he complained not.

A terrible loss to the community of environmental scholars, of whom he was a leader, mentor, and guide. He worked hard to articulate through paths in the intricate and overgrown area of environmental law that worked and made sense to many of his colleagues, and were built upon and expanded by them, and will continue to be. A terrible loss to his future students, who will not have the benefit of his magical admixture of deep knowledge, skilled teaching, and warm affection which he freely offered to all of the several thousand students he did touch during his time at Denver Law. Here is a picture of Fred, speaking with a student at a faculty advising event a few months before he died, which offers well more than a thousand words of his genuine loving engagement with students.

Photo by Wayne Armstrong

Some said of Fred that he had become the consummate Westerner. Riding his bike to work every day—which one student described to me after his death as "righteous"—and hiking the paths and rafting the rivers of Colorado, which he did often. But there were two people, at least, who knew this was mostly wishful thinking and mere adaptation. As two exiled New Yorkers, we knew better. As he said of us: we weren't Westerners and never would be, we were "refugees." One of my many sorrows about his death is that Fred will no longer be able to glory in the natural world of our adopted state which he had come to love doing so much.

Each layer of immense loss is a reason alone to dedicate this book to Fred, but none of them are why I am doing so. This book is dedicated to Fred because, simply put, without him it would probably not exist. As a second-class citizen of the academy, I have often been overlooked and underestimated as a scholar, and as I switched from practicing law to teaching it, I bought in to much of that view. But it was Fred who saw the first book in my work and thinking—*Law School 2.0: Legal Education for a Digital Age* (2009)—and prodded me to write it. And I dedicated it to him in gratitude for his insistence that I write it and for giving me the confidence that I could. When I was nearly finished with it, he reviewed a draft manuscript and made a few suggestions, but mostly he just said this: "You have found your voice."

In the intervening years, as law schools entered their decade of significant trial—after the Great Recession that started just as the book went to press, and more recently, responding to Covid—and while he served as our Associate Dean for Academic Affairs, he continued to encourage me and hear me out on further ideas that I had about the future of legal education. He read links I sent him, and he sent me some himself. We discussed the maelstrom of attacks on legal education and some of the wild suggestions for its improvement over innumerable end-of-day meetings over a beer. He continued to prod me to write this book: the follow up to *Law School 2.0*, but a significant expansion of it. He was disappointed it was taking so long. I had several articles and two textbook updates to do first, and he was still impatient. I was still working out my thinking on some of these issues, and he was still impatient. I probably got impatient with him for being impatient with me. "It matters what we get on paper, David," he would say. So, we continued to meet almost every week and discuss life and politics and the law school and the university, and this book.

Fred has been gone several years as I write this dedication, and there is quite a bit of thinking in this book that I never got to sufficiently discuss with him. In some ways, in parts of this book I am partially writing *to* Fred. Sometimes, when we met for a beer, he would—as a good colleague should—challenge my thinking, and on some level I would walk away believing I had not gotten through, that he did not fully understand what I was trying to say. We certainly did not agree on everything. And then he would occasionally offer Zen koans like this: "I have seen the future, David, and it involves more of you than it does of me." He was speaking of more contract faculty and fewer tenured faculty on law faculties of the future. Or was he?

So, this book is dedicated to Fred because I miss my friend and colleague, and because I loved him, and because it would not exist without him, but also—and finally—because it completes a more than ten-year conversation I had with him. Everything I have is in it, Fred. I hope I still have my voice. I am devastated beyond measure that we have lost yours.

Acknowledgments

No book of any size or worth comes together without the support to the author offered by many others.

One of the smartest things I have done in my life is to ask my wife Kathy to marry me, and I am blessed beyond measure that she said yes. This book is also dedicated to her. Our daughters Angelina and Sarah-Jane have blessed the two of us every day of their lives. For me, the foundation of family has allowed me the base from which to think and to write, and I am deeply grateful to them for that, and so much more.

I have many colleagues—in addition to Fred—who have acted as supports and sounding boards for so much of what you will find in this book. Among them are Cliff Zimmerman (Northwestern), Ian Gallacher (Syracuse), Carol Wallinger (Rutgers), Steve Daniels (ABF), Paul Maharg (Osgood), Wan Meng (Beijing FSU), Svetlana Tyulkina (New South Wales), Greg Brandes (St. Francis), Sara Berman (Touro), Akira Fujimoto (Nagoya), Linda Edwards (UNLV), Varvara Maslova (Moscow State), my colleagues at Denver Law Marty Katz, Roberto Corrada, and Scott Johns, and judges Bob McGahey and Russ Carparelli. I am profoundly grateful to them all. I am especially grateful to Ian and Carol for providing comments on an earlier draft, and to Steve for sourcing the data for the tuition calculations in Chapter Eight.

My earliest work on this book was developed while I was hosted as Visiting Scholar at the Institute for the Advancement of the American Legal System (IAALS) in 2013 during a sabbatical. While there, I had the privilege of working with Bill Sullivan, Rebecca Kourlis, Logan Cornett, and the late Alli Gerkman. I am grateful to IAALS for giving me workspace during that semester, and for our many collaborations around the Educating Tomorrow's Lawyers project.

Most of my scholarship over the last fifteen years has centered around the topics addressed in this book, so it is not surprising that it contains some excerpts from articles first published in law reviews. All of the excerpts are included here with permission of the journals that originally printed them, and I am grateful to the editorial staffs of each of them: the Syracuse Law Review, the St. Louis University Law Journal, the Journal of Law and Education, Perspectives, the Journal of Experiential Learning, Regent University Law Review, and Elgar Publishing.

All of my thinking on this book has been informed by my nearly 1,000 students at the University of Denver in the last 25 years. I have learned so much by working with them. Truly everything you read here was influenced by my experiences with my students, who each and every one—even the occasionally difficult ones—have blessed me with their attention.

Among those students, I am particularly indebted to my teaching and research assistants over the years. I have been immeasurably lucky to get to know even better those who have stepped up to assist in my work, whether teaching or writing (or both). Among those are Megan Embrey, Kendra Beckwith, Chad Grell, Nicole King, Ian London, Katy Mika, Cody Barela, Kelsey Covert, Megan McCulloch, Jeff Sparhawk, Ellen Blatt, Thomas Galloway, and Kelsey Wilcox.

I am also blessed with incredible research support from our faculty support librarians over the years, particularly Diane Burkhardt and Michelle Penn. I am grateful to my publisher, Carolina Academic Press, and their support of my work over the years since they took my books over from LexisNexis.

Finally, I am grateful to my in-laws, Flora Rodriguez Russel and the late Dan Russel, who made their Casita in Santa Fe available to me over the last 15 years so that I could get away for periods of unstructured writing time. This book would likely not exist without that simple gift.

THE WAY FORWARD FOR LEGAL EDUCATION →

ONE

The Worrisome State of the Profession and the Academy

Introduction

It would be hard to argue today that the way forward for legal education is the same as what we have been doing—the status quo—for many significant reasons. First, there have been decades of criticism of legal education, much of it well founded. Second, the law school student population does not mirror the population at large, and thus the profession does not either. Third, it has become apparent that legal education must play a greater role in restoring our democratic institutions. Fourth, there are vast numbers of unmet legal needs in our society, and a lack of equal access to the justice system. Fifth, too many students are graduating with crushing debt burdens. Finally, the massive disruption caused by the Covid pandemic changed legal education in ways we are just discovering.

But the criticism of the structure of legal education continues. The institution must be equally accessible to those historically blocked entry. Access to justice is a critical issue—lawyers have priced themselves out of addressing many legal needs. Lawyers and teachers of law have an important role in restoring the legitimacy of our democratic institutions, and if we do not engage in that fight, there will be little need for law schools in that dystopian future. Outside of the top schools feeding (largely) corporate law, the student debt problem is nearing the existential. And the COVID-19 pandemic taught us that with some effort, we have the tools and ability to open up the brick walls of the institution and reach a larger, more diverse audience.

Each of these elements have reached an inflection point. We need to prepare for and activate changes to address these elements for the betterment of the institution. We need to build a clear path forward so that legal education not just survives, but thrives, in the future.

This diagram illustrates the forces currently pressing on the legal profession and legal education.

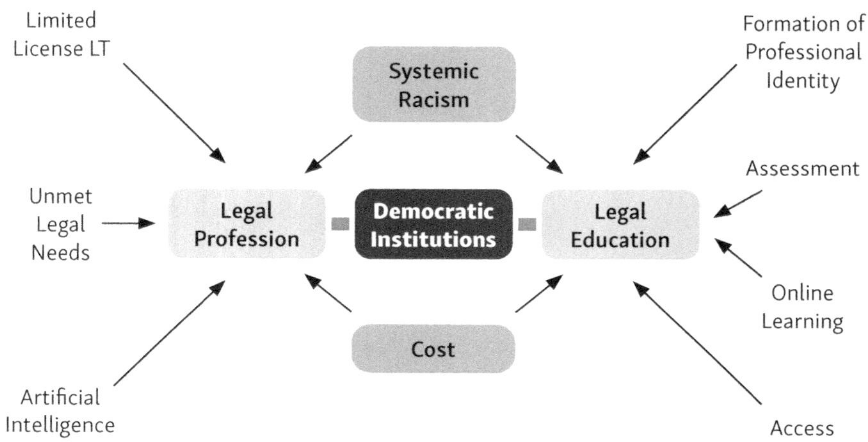

The Legal Profession

We sometimes lose sight of this, but in legal education we serve the profession of law by providing new lawyers to join it. As a result of that obvious fact, it is important that we are knowledgeable about the pressures on the profession, particularly those that are likely to change and improve it. Because if it is going to change in ways that matter, what we offer our students should also change. If not, we are producing new lawyers prepared for the legal profession of our past, not their future.

Perhaps the greatest threat to the legitimacy of the legal profession today is the vast unmet legal need in our society.[1] If the profession merely serves corpo-

1. Brittany Kauffman & Logan Cornett, *Report on Justice Needs and Satisfaction in the United States of America*, IAALS (Sept. 1, 2021), https://iaalsdu.edu/sites/default/files/documents/publications/justice-needs-and-satisfaction-us.pdf. The report indicated that 66 percent of respondents had a legal problem in the last four years, and of those only 49 percent

rate interests and the monied class that can pay its bills, it deserves some of the derision and lack of faith it receives. Yes, we have public defenders, radically underfunded as they are. But on the civil side, what do we offer? Some clinics in law schools. Some pro-bono work supported by law firms. And not much else. And so potential clients go to LegalZoom and Rocket Lawyer, and get a sub-standard product and learn that law can be simplified, leading inexorably to the conclusion: who needs lawyers? One of the greatest tragedies in law over the last fifty years is that we have lost or degraded the social service orientation that all lawyers should have, and law schools bear some responsibility for that.

In response to these unmet legal needs, some states have been experimenting with non-lawyer certification in a specialty area—such as family law—that provides quasi-legal services to those cases that do not require a fully licensed lawyer. These are known as Limited License Legal Technicians (LLLTs). To the lasting shame of the legal profession—which also serves to undermine trust of the general public—these efforts have so far been resisted and voted down in many states. But several states have persisted, and experimented, and some progress is being made. If such a trend continues—and this book argues that it should and likely will—law schools have an opportunity to serve a new market of students who seek a cheaper and shorter certification that gets them to the LLLT. The lower fees they will charge for their services will be manageable with lower debt loads, since they will only need to attend law school for one year.

Whether in industry or education, it is fashionable to predict the latest earth-shattering change looming just out of sight on the horizon. A recent example has been the potential impact of Artificial Intelligence (AI) on the practice of law, and by implication, legal education. It is certainly true that AI is having an impact on many industries, and it will impact law as well.[2] But the dystopian visions of the "Robot Lawyer" overseeing a vastly restructured legal landscape are overblown.[3] We should be mindful that AI has a long history—at least forty years long—of a predicted profound impact that mostly has never come to pass.[4]

were completely resolved. "This is a crisis that demands increased advocacy and funding for policies and services that increase access to justice across broad segments of society." *Id.*

2. *See, e.g.*, Julie Sobowale, *How Artificial Intelligence is Transforming the Legal Profession*, A.B.A. J., (Apr. 1, 2016, 12:10 AM) http://www.abajournal.com/magazine/article/how_artificial_intelligence_is_transforming_the_legal_profession.

3. Others agree, at least for now. *See* Steve Lohr, *A.I. Is Doing Legal Work. But it Won't Replace Lawyers. Yet.*, NY Times, Mar. 29, 2017, at B1.

4. *See* Tanya Lewis, *A Brief History of Artificial Intelligence*, Live Sci. (Dec. 4, 2014), https://www.livescience.com/49007-history-of-artificial-intelligence.html. The field of AI

It does seem more than likely that some repetitive aspects of legal practice will be improved and made more efficient with technology, and indeed this has already happened, such as in the area of litigation document discovery. Over the last decade, there has been an explosion in the discovery of relevant documents in electronic format, and technology has made a significant improvement in speed and efficiency in this space. In particular, the application of Technology Assisted Review (TAR) in litigation is making significant improvements to document productions in electronic format, and the application of machine learning will likely continue to do so.[5]

But this shift is more likely a "shift up" in the types of work that lawyers do and will not gut the substance. There are routinized things that lawyers do, without much thought or nuance. Those can be automated. Forms for simple transactions can be (and have been) automated, making the work of a LLLT more efficient. So, lawyers in the future will rely on intelligent assistants, which will allow them to focus on more substantively complex work that the multivariate business world of the future will likely require. Lawyers will not be replaced by robots, but rather work alongside various forms of AI doing more advanced work than is typical today. This will have impacts on the profession in certain areas, moving lawyers up the "thought pyramid" to higher level work. Legal education will need to adjust to these changes and need to prepare for a legal world assisted, but not replaced, by artificial intelligence.

Of greater immediate concern is the increasing threats to our democratic institutions that have occurred in the United States over the last decade. Among these are attempts to dismantle the "administrative state," limits on voting rights that are often targeted at reducing the minority voice, and even a direct attack on the functioning of our government in January of 2021. Many of these attacks seem to be racially motivated, directly or indirectly. But they are also the product of failure and fear. Many citizens of this country have lost

---

was formally founded in 1956, but has experienced many intervals of inactivity; research and funding have been more steady since 1997 when IBM's computer, Deep Blue, defeated chess champion Garry Kasparov. *See also* Lee Bell, *AI Will Play a Vital Role in our Future, Just Don't Expect Robot Butlers*, The Inquirer (Mar. 14, 2014), https://www.theinquirer.net/inquirer/opinion/2334325/will-robots-play-a-vital-role-in-our-future (noting that AI software "is running underneath all sorts of modern technological tasks from autopilot to the . . . gyroscope ability of Segways," but we are far from the long-anticipated "servant droids.").

5. *See, e.g.*, James A. Sherer et al., *Court Guideposts for the Path to Technology Assisted Review Adoption*, 35 Comput. & Internet L. 1, 1–2 (2018).

faith that the government is not designed and targeted to undermine their interests—it has failed them, and they are fearful as a result. While many elite members of the legal profession might like to write these citizens off as crazies—or fringe members of society in some way—we now know we do that at our peril. There are forces outside this country who would like to see our democracy fail, and there are many inside this country who believe the only way they will be represented is to tear it down and start over. The best response to these understandable fears is to reassess and reconstruct those institutions that are engaged in upholding and perpetuating our system of government.

One of those central institutions is the legal system and the lawyers and judges who uphold it. Since the legal profession is not serving all those who need it ("the justice gap"), and the judiciary seems remote to many and subject to political pressure, there is a critical need to shore up these aspects of the foundation upon which our country is built and how it functions. Legal education is where all those principles are born and instilled in students, and so a reassessment and re-construction of legal education stressing professional formation that has shifted toward making it more egalitarian and more focused towards service to the public will over time contribute to the strengthening of our democratic institutions.

The most devastating charge against the legal profession, and our law schools, is that of its role in perpetuating systemic racism. In many states, lawyers take an oath of office at their swearing-in ceremony to improve the legal profession. But while there have been decades of "blue-ribbon" panels at local bar associations concerned about this issue and various "diversity pipeline" efforts, little changes. The percentage of BIPOC partners in law firms across the country is vastly smaller than the population.[6] A recent study by the American Bar Association (ABA) showed that 2.1 percent of law firm partners are black and showed an increase of just 0.4 percent in that number since 2010.[7] The overall conclusion of this latest survey is that, once again, white males land law firm partnerships at the fastest rates, despite the increase of female members of the profession.[8]

The profession of law misses out on so much because of this—we have a poorer profession because we are less than we could be and should be. Citizens

6. *A.B.A. Profile of the Legal Profession 2020*, A.B.A., July 2020, at 33; *2021 A.B.A. Model Diversity Survey*, A.B.A., July 2021, at 10.

7. *Id.*

8. *Id.*

all over the country need legal help and feel locked out and cannot find lawyers who look like them. Law firms have two main responses to this issue: first, they admit that there is such a thing as "fit" to the law and to the culture of the firm,[9] which is just an admission that the current makeup of law firm partners is racism weakly justified, and it is wrong. Second, they blame law schools for not graduating enough BIPOC students. In this charge, they are right.

The Legal Education System We Have

Legal education, for the most part, knows what it needs to do to improve, it just does not want to. The American Bar Association, which accredits law schools, is increasingly using the accreditation standards to force change. Among its efforts are those around Assessment, the Formation of Professional Identity, and the support of Online Learning. Each of these has the potential to change legal education substantially.

It might seem odd to an outsider, but law professors have little incentive to be excellent teachers. As a result, they are—as a group—rarely current on methods of assessment that are standard in most undergraduate institutions. Thus, it must be sufficient to advance their students' learning to having one summative exam at the end of the semester, and perhaps even in the form of a multiple-choice test that is quicker to grade. The evidence that this sort of testing is not ideal or fair is overwhelming, and yet it continues.[10] But the ABA now requires an assessment plan in each law school and seems to hope that this will eventually trickle down into each course.[11]

When the *Carnegie Report* on Legal Education was published in 2007[12] it introduced the concept of the Formation of Professional Identity and charged that law schools were not doing enough to support this formation. There was—and perhaps still is—confusion about what this referred to. After all, the ABA requires the class in professional responsibility, and every law school

---

9. *Foundations for Practice: Survey Overview and Methodological Approach*, IAALS, Univ. Denv., July 26, 2016, https://iaals.du.edu/publications/foundations-practice-survey-overview-and-methodological-approach.

10. Rogelio A. Lasso, *Is Our Students Learning? Using Assessments to Measure and Improve Law School Learning and Performance*, 15 Barry L. Rev. 73, 79–82 (2010).

11. A.B.A. Section of Legal Educ. & Admission to the Bar, Standards and Rules of Procedure for Approval of Law Schools 2021–2022, Ch. 3 (2021).

12. William M. Sullivan et al., Educating Lawyers: Preparation for the Profession of Law (John Wiley & Sons, Inc. 2007) [hereinafter Carnegie Report].

teaches it. But what the *Carnegie Report* was referring to was something else: that law students should be given intentional opportunities to decide what sort of lawyer they were going to be. To build their own identity in the law, not necessarily the predominantly white male identity they mostly saw in their classrooms.[13] And to decide where they would place themselves above the ethical line defined by the rules. Individual law professors have been grappling ever since with how to go about providing opportunities for students to do this.

The access issue presses on legal education more urgently every day. If we are merely an elite institution for the elite—something most of those involved in legal education would like to vehemently deny—then we deserve the criticism we receive. We rely heavily on—and our rankings depend heavily on—the Law School Admissions Test. This is a known discriminatory instrument,[14] and we have known this for a long time.[15] With the goal of being reliable and repeatable, it tests quick thinking, when much good lawyering involves slow thinking. The LSAT must be removed as a criterion for admission and the law school admissions process must be overhauled. Yes, that means the creation of holistic models for admission, and that will make it much harder to do well, but undoubtedly fairer.[16] Despite the best efforts of many law school deans over many years, this simply will not change with an ever-elusive mix of financial aid and other incentives. As long as law school rankings are heavily influenced by a discriminatory instrument, we will remain an institution that perpetuates

13. Bennett Capers, *The Law School as a White Space*, 106 Minn. L. Rev. 7, 22–26 (2021); *See also* Carrie Yang Costello, Crisis in Professional Identity Crisis: Race, Class, Gender, and Success at Professional Schools (Vanderbilt Univ. Press 2005).

14. Aaron N. Taylor, *The Marginalization of Aspiring Black Lawyers*, 13 FIU L. Rev. 489, 505–506 (2019);

15. *See* James C. Hathaway, *The Mythical Meritocracy of Law School Admissions*, 34 J. Legal Educ. 86 (1984).

16. There have been some criticisms of the ABA's proposal to remove the requirement for a standardized test for admission to law school. Vivia Chen, *Killing the LSAT in the Name of Diversity Won't Cure the Problem*, US Law Week, June 24, 2022, https://news.bloomberglaw.com/us-law-week/killing-the-lsat-in-the-name-of-diversity-wont-cure-the-problem. The criticism suggests that the discriminatory effect of the LSAT will just be replaced with discrimination based on schools attended, majors studied, etc. Obviously, that would be a net negative. But it does not *have* to be that way as there is research available about how we might go about developing a better approach. *See, e.g.*, Marjorie M. Shultz & Sheldon Zedick, *Admission to Law School: New Measures*, 47 Educ. Psychol. 51 (2012); *See also*, Hathaway, *supra* n. 15 (advocating for a "goal-oriented admissions policy").

systemic racism. And the legal profession will have a convenient excuse for its abysmal record on creating an integrated profession.[17]

Worse, when law schools do admit BIPOC students with what they perceive to be sufficient LSAT scores, they are typically in such small numbers that many struggle with being an outsider and have feelings of not belonging there.[18] A sense of belonging is particularly important during the time of a student's life when they are transitioning to a profession.[19] But law schools are not an even playing field for all students.[20] When students are trying to join a profession that is built on notions of justice and fairness, and yet are subjected to bias and stereotype concerns during their law school experience, it undermines the entire enterprise for them.[21]

The judiciary retains the responsibility for the bar examination—its design and administration. And it too bears much blame for perpetuating systemic racism in the legal profession. Like the LSAT, it seeks the goal of being reliable and repeatable, and thus a "valid" testing instrument. But the problem is focusing on memorization of testable topics and this distorts the entire enterprise. So, while a broad understanding of foundational principles of Constitutional Law and Civil Procedure and Property Law are no doubt important, much time is spent in those courses (and many others) teaching topics that are testable but have little relevance in practice. And—like the LSAT—it once again rewards speed, and those who have had the privilege of years of high-level educational practice with this sort of measurement are rewarded. Thus, the system perpetuates itself. The bar examination must be overhauled to focus on the stated goal: preparation for the practice of law, not the skill of taking high speed tests.

The cost issue for the legal profession and legal education is different in nature. For legal education, it is the overall cost of attendance at law school,

---

17. A. Benjamin Spencer, *Law Schools, Law Firms Must Share Responsibility for Diversity*, Bloomberglaw.com (July 21, 2021, 2:00 AM), https://news.bloomberglaw.com/bankruptcy-law/law-schools-law-firms-must-share-responsibility-for-diversity.

18. Elizabeth Bodamer, *Do I Belong Here? Examining Perceived Experiences of Bias, Stereotype Concerns, and Sense of Belonging in U.S. Law Schools*, 69 J. Legal Educ. 455, 456–57 (2010).

19. *Id.* at 456.

20. Elizabeth Mertz, *Inside the Law School Classroom: Toward a New Realist Pedagogy*, 60 Vand. L. Rev. 483, 511 (2007); *see also*, Elizabeth Mertz, The Language of Law School: Learning to "Think Like a Lawyer" 222 (Oxford Univ. Press, 2007).

21. *See* Bodamer, *supra* note 18, at 460, 462.

which for many students includes living expenses, and little or no pay during summer jobs (often denoted "internships") in the law. The cost of a law degree, for many students, is in the range of $130,000–$180,000.[22] These costs vary for public versus private schools, but that gap has been narrowing in recent years.[23] The overall cost, with interest over 10 years, can exceed $300,000. If all legal jobs offered salaries in the $200,000 range perhaps this would not be a problem. But most do not. Average salaries are in the $65,000 range in most markets. Thus, a graduate can be saddled with a monthly payment of $1,800 per month for 10 years. At some point, this can become more of a moral question than a math question. Some law professors might think that is the equivalent of a mortgage and fail to see the consequences. But that graduate may not be able to afford a mortgage after paying off that debt burden every month. They are often forced to work in a law firm and it limits choices they can make about their early careers.

The truly elite law schools—by reputation—can charge whatever they like, as they send many of their graduates to those $200,000 jobs. But most law schools serve much smaller, local, markets and salaries do not reach that level for many years and may not even then. So, if the premise that you can attend law school and reach or remain in the upper middle class breaks down, what do we offer then? In recognition of the seriousness of student indebtedness, the U.S. News law school rankings now factor it in to their rankings. This alone is a strong incentive to lower tuition costs at all but the top schools.

About the cost of legal education, and its relationship to legal education's access issue, Justice O'Connor said this in *Grutter v. Bollinger*: "Access to legal education (and thus the legal profession) must be inclusive of talented and qualified individuals of every race and ethnicity, so that all members of our heterogeneous society may participate in the educational institutions that provide the training and education necessary to succeed in America."[24]

Bringing the cost down is essential, but not easy. Educational costs are high at all levels and the university cost structure depends on that not changing

---

22. Melanie Hanson, *Average Cost of Law School*, Educationdata.org (Nov. 30, 2021), https://educationdata.org/average-cost-of-law-school.

23. *Id.* The *average* cumulative amount borrowed (in 2020 dollars) by law school graduates in 2016 was $126,200 and 71 percent of law students took on debt at some level. *AccessLex Legal Education Data Deck*, p. 23, 31 (Apr. 2022). https://www.accesslex.org/sites/default/files/2022-06/AccessLex%20Legal%20Education%20Data%20Deck%20-%2005-26-2022.pdf.

24. *Grutter v. Bollinger*, 539 U.S. 306, 332–33 (2003).

radically. Fortunately, there is a solution, and it is found in online teaching and learning that we learned so much about during the pandemic. Legal education must serve more students at lower cost by delivering online and hybrid learning during the law school years, particularly the first year.

The Criticism of Legal Education

Legal education has been criticized for over a hundred years,[25] but in the last thirty years, a series of reports has contained criticism and suggestions for improvement. The first report of the modern era was issued in 1992 by a panel of practicing lawyers and legal educators brought together in 1989 by the Council of the Section of Legal Education and Admissions to the Bar at the American Bar Association.[26] The colloquial name for this report comes from the chair of that panel, Robert MacCrate, a prominent attorney in New York.[27] The *MacCrate Report* offered a list of ten "Skills" and four "Values" that it concluded were fundamental to proper training for the practice of law.[28] This list became a guideline for curricular reform at many law schools in the 1990s, and in particular, was the genesis of significant growth in the clinical legal education movement.[29] However, much of that growth was focused on the ten lawyering skills that the *MacCrate Report* listed, which included problem solving; legal research, analysis, and reasoning; written and oral communication; client counseling; negotiation; and recognizing and resolving ethical dilemmas.[30] The *MacCrate Report* had significant impact on the development and

---

25. *See* Josef Redlich, The Common Law and the Case Method in American University Law Schools: A Report to the Carnegie Foundation for the Advancement of Teaching (1914); Alfred Zantzinger Reed, Training for the Public Profession of the Law xiv–xv (1921). Portions of this chapter were previously published in David I. C. Thomson, *How Online Learning Will Transform Legal Education, in* Research Handbook on Digital Transformations (F. Xavier Olleros and Majlinda Zhegu, eds. Elgar 2016), and are reprinted here with permission.

26. A.B.A Task Force on Law Schs. & Profession: Narrowing the Gap, *Legal Education & Professional Development—An Educational Continuum*, at xi–xiv (1992) [hereinafter *MacCrate Report*].

27. *See* Catherine L. Carpenter, A Survey of Law School Curricula: 2002–2010 1 (2012).

28. *MacCrate Report*, *supra* note 26, at 138–41.

29. *See* Wallace Loh, *Introduction: The MacCrate Report—Heuristic or Prescriptive?*, 69 Wash. L. Rev. 505, 514–15 (1994); *see also* Bryant G. Garth, *From MacCrate to Carnegie: Very Different Movements for Curricular Reform*, 17 J. Legal Writing Inst. 261, 264 (2011).

30. *MacCrate Report*, *supra* note 26, at 138–40.

expansion of clinical legal education, as well as the expansion of skills classes including legal writing.[31] Less noticed, and less implemented, was the "Values" portion of the recommendations. But the *MacCrate Report* also endorsed four "Fundamental Values of the Profession": (1) Provision of Competent Representation; (2) Striving to Promote Justice, Fairness, and Morality; (3) Striving to Improve the Profession; and (4) Professional Self-Development.[32]

Much of law school is focused on the first value: competent representation.[33] But there is much else of importance in this list. There is a reference to the morality of the profession, and the list includes such goals as promoting justice and fairness and a commitment to improvement of the profession, as well as one's own professional self-development.[34] Because the primary focus of law school is on learning the law to represent the interests of a client,[35] what remains in this list of professional values are only occasionally or indirectly addressed.

Starting in the late 1990s, the Carnegie Foundation for the Advancement of Teaching initiated a wide-ranging study of professional education in several fields.[36] The project, called Preparation for the Professions, included studies of medical, clergy, engineering, and legal education, and each project issued an extensive report.[37] The report on legal education, entitled *Educating Lawyers: Preparation for the Profession of Law*, was published in 2007.[38] The three principal contributions of the *Carnegie Report* for legal education were: first, that it identified the "three apprenticeships" of effective legal training;[39] second, that it argued strongly in favor of the integration of all three appren-

31. *See* Garth, *supra* note 29, at 264.

32. *MacCrate Report, supra* note 26, at 140–41.

33. *See id.* at 210–12 (noting that the goal of competent representation is recognized in the A.B.A.'s Model Rules of Professional Conduct and the A.B.A.'s Code of Professional Conduct).

34. *MacCrate Report, supra* note 26, at 140–41.

35. *See* A.B.A. Section of Legal Educ. & Admission to the Bar, A.B.A. Standards and Rules of Procedure for Approval of Law Schools 2014–2015, Standard 302 (2014).

36. *See* Neil Hamilton, *Fostering Professional Formation (Professionalism): Lessons from the Carnegie Foundation's Five Studies on Educating Professionals*, 45 Creighton L. Rev. 763, 765 (2012).

37. Carnegie Report, *supra* note 12, at 15. For a brief description of these reports, *see* Hamilton, *supra* note 27, at 769–71.

38. *See generally* Carnegie Report, *supra* note 12, at 27.

39. *Id.*

ticeships throughout legal education;[40] and third, that it brought attention to the importance of professional identity formation.[41] The three apprenticeships it identified in the report were: (1) the cognitive, (2) the practical, and (3) the ethical-social.[42] The cognitive apprenticeship focuses on what has long been referred to as "thinking like a lawyer."[43] The practical apprenticeship focuses on practical lawyering skills and harkens back to the list of skills in the *MacCrate Report*.[44] The ethical-social apprenticeship focuses on the formation of the student as a professional attorney.[45]

The *Carnegie Report* found that law schools were generally effective, particularly in the first year, inculcating in students the principles of the first apprenticeship through the case method of study, which it called the "signature pedagog[y]" in law school.[46] Concerning the practical apprenticeship, the report expressed concern that there was not enough teaching of legal doctrine in the context of practice, noting that "[w]ith little or no direct exposure to the experience of practice, students have slight basis on which to distinguish between the demands of actual practice and the peculiar requirements of law school."[47] In this way, the *Carnegie Report* refocused attention on skills needed for practice, as the *MacCrate Report* did before it.[48]

However, the *Carnegie Report* reserved its greatest criticism of legal education for the lack of intentional development of its students in the third apprenticeship, the ethical-social, which it also referred to as the students' formation of professional identity as a lawyer.[49] In recent years, conferences and

40. *See id.* at 28–29.

41. *See id.* at 14.

42. *See id.* at 28.

43. *Id.*

44. *See MacCrate Report, supra* note 26, at 138–41.

45. Carnegie Report, *supra* note 12, at 28, 123.

46. *Id.* at 2, 23–28.

47. *Id.* at 95.

48. *Compare id.* (noting that the key to becoming an effective legal problem-solver is practicing legal problem-solving in real or hypothetical situations), *with MacCrate Report, supra* note 26, at 138–141 (identifying ten fundamental lawyering skills).

49. *See* Carnegie Report, *supra* note 12, at 145–152. The *Carnegie Report* likely used the word "identity" quite intentionally. The psychologist Erik Erikson developed the concept of identity in the middle of the twentieth century. Howard Gardner et al., Good Work: When Excellence and Ethics Meet 11 (Basic Books 2001). Identity has been defined as a combination of "a person's deeply felt convictions about who she is, and what matters most to her existence as a worker, a citizen, and a human being." *Id.* Contemporaries summarized

commentators have begun to focus on this apprenticeship—what it means and what sorts of adjustments to legal education might be needed to address it.[50] Bryant Garth, former Director of the American Bar Foundation and dean at two law schools, has suggested that this recommendation, and the changes it will bring if taken seriously, may have an even more profound impact on legal education than the *MacCrate Report* has had.[51]

Among the *Carnegie Report*'s most important recommendations were that the three apprenticeships should be integrated throughout the law school course of study, and that paying greater attention to the third apprenticeship could help facilitate that integration.[52] Even the report itself mentions the potential power of law schools paying significant attention to the third apprenticeship: "The third element of the framework—professional identity—joins the first two elements and is, we believe, *the catalyst* for an integrated legal education."[53] The report criticized the typical law school curriculum as being too separated between doctrine and skills and recommended that law schools make an effort to integrate all three apprenticeships into their curricula.[54]

> A more adequate and properly formative legal education requires a better balance among the cognitive, practical, and ethical-social apprenticeships. To achieve this balance, legal educators will have to do more than shuffle the existing pieces. The problem demands their careful rethinking of both the existing curriculum and the pedagogies that

---

Erikson's theory of identity formation as follows: "Each person's identity is shaped by an amalgam of forces, including family history, religious and ideological beliefs, community membership, and idiosyncratic individual experiences." *Id.*

50. For example, the first annual conference of the Educating Tomorrow's Lawyers initiative of IAALS, which took place September 27–29, 2012, was thematically focused on the third apprenticeship. *See Event: The Development of Professional Identity*, Educating Tomorrow's Lawyers, http://educatingtomorrowslawyers.du.edu/events/the-development-of-professional-identity-in-legal-education-rethinking-lear/program/. Also, at the Southeastern Association of Law Schools (SEALS) 2014 Conference, a three-hour discussion group of ten law faculty addressed itself to a detailed discussion of the third apprenticeship and prepared short papers on the subject in advance. *See Seals 2014 Conference Program*, SEALS, http://sealslawschools.org/submissions/program/pastprograms.asp?confyear=2014.

51. *See* Garth, *supra* note 29, at 267.

52. Carnegie Report, *supra* note 12, at 28. For a broader discussion of the concept of formation of professional identity and how to support it in the law school curriculum, see Chapter 3.

53. *Id.* at 14 (emphasis added).

54. *See id.* at 27–29.

law schools employ to produce a more coherent and integrated initiation into a life in the law.[55]

The report further argues that the apprenticeship of professionalism and purpose should be *subordinated* to the cognitive, academic apprenticeship."[56] In the same year that the *Carnegie Report* was published, the Clinical Legal Education Association (CLEA) published its own report on legal education, entitled *Best Practices for Legal Education: A Vision and A Road Map*.[57] This report called on law schools "to make a commitment to improve the preparation of their students for practice, clarify and expand their educational objectives, improve and diversify the methods for delivering instruction, and give more attention to evaluating the success of their programs of instruction."[58] Chapter Four of the Best Practices report provided a comprehensive guide for law teaching at its best and most well designed. Like the *Carnegie Report*, the Best Practices report endorsed pactice-based instruction to support the integration of doctrine and skills training.[59]

Conclusion

The legal profession and the legal education system that serves it are both at an inflection point. The way forward is unclear and muddling through seems to be the default, majority approach. As Dean Megan Carpenter has expressed it: "For many law schools, the old way of doing things, frankly, does not present a sustainable business model."[60] But to address all these concerns—and the lengthy, detailed criticism directed at law schools for decades—we need a new model for legal education. This book attempts to offer it.

---

55. *Id.* at 147.

56. *Id.* at 132–33 (emphasis added).

57. Roy Stuckey, Best Practices for Legal Education: A Vision and a Road Map (Jossey-Bass 2007) [hereinafter Best Practices Report].

58. *Id.* at 7.

59. *Id.* at 146–53.

60. Megan M. Carpenter, *Legal Education Unbundled (and Rebundled)*, 50 U. Tol. L. Rev. 265, 272 (2019).

TWO

The Old and New Models for Legal Education

The Old Model

To be sure, legal education has made significant changes over the last few decades—partly in reaction to the criticism it has received—and mostly for the better. There have been additions of clinics, experiential learning opportunities, and the significant expansion of externship programs. But the basic model of legal education, created largely by Christopher Columbus Langdell, the first Dean of Harvard Law School[1] has remained largely in place. We still have the six or seven "doctrinal courses" in the first year, taught mostly siloed from each other, with a summative examination at the end holding the full grade weight for the semester. Some of those tests are even still multiple-choice, so they can be graded without intervention of the professor and providing little in the way of feedback (other than the grade). While students can review their exam with their professor, they are usually not allowed to contest a grade so they rarely bother. These classes are large, typically sixty to ninety students in number, and it is difficult for the professor to get to know each student personally. That—combined with the prevailing pedagogy—make student engagement low and motivated mostly by fear of the grade and of being called on in class. While those professors hold office hours, students sometimes get the idea that the professor does not want to spend the time answering pesky 1L questions, and stop coming.

1. William Schofield, *Christopher Columbus Langdell*, 55 U. Pa. L. Rev. 273, 273 (1907).

The legal writing course is one of two required by the ABA to be in the curriculum—the other is the legal ethics course—and it is here that students get to know their professors well and also their peers. Legal writing is a difficult course to teach well and an easy one to teach poorly, so it is important that schools professionalize their legal writing faculty and pay them equitably and give them a voice in the governance of the law school. Progress is being made on these points. But what these professors do is not well known in the academy. Their role in helping their students lay a solid foundation for the rest of law school and their legal careers is not well understood. Because the primary teaching methodology of the course is experiential learning, this will be addressed in Chapter Four.

In second and third year, the curriculum opens up for our students. They have many options and are sometimes bewildered by them. Faculty advising is often poor. The practice-focused courses are often taught by adjuncts—not professional teachers—and smaller seminars are offered by the faculty in their area of specialty. This affords students a better opportunity to get to know a non-legal writing faculty member, and sometimes this leads to opportunities for joint research. As students progress through these years, they gradually specialize in an area of law and integrate summer jobs and externships into their learning.

Also during second and third year—and as part of this specialization—students apply for and some are admitted to clinical opportunities for learning, where they represent clients under the supervision of a clinical professor. These can be invaluable learning opportunities for our students, but they are not available to all because clinical opportunities in most law schools are a limited resource.

The University

Most law schools are part of a larger university, and they depend on the tuition income provided by their law schools because the majority of universities are not heavily endowed. Those that are may not have to be quite as concerned about the future of legal education. But the rest must work unceasingly to stay ahead of their competition or suffer the consequences. They can do this by advancing a culture of innovation, and by enabling their faculty to increase the impact of the educational programs they offer. While increasing value they must, where possible, decrease cost. Costs have simply gotten out of hand in the last two decades and the reduction in legislative funding for public universities has only exacerbated the situation.

Important to the future of higher education will be exploring the nature, techniques, and outcomes for providing a more customized learning experience for our students. We know we want to treat each student as an individual—not a fungible widget—and we usually succeed in meeting that goal. But there are emerging technologies that can help us follow their progress and support our students as the individuals they are that go well beyond traditional faculty advising, which is already lacking. Where it is not, students notice such efforts immediately.

Despite massive change in how many students will achieve the undergraduate degree across the country (and online), there will remain enduring value in a high-quality residential undergraduate experience. It may own a shrinking percentage of the market, but it retains great value for those who can afford it. However, as other options proliferate, universities must remain vigilant to preserve and enhance that value.

In the in-person setting, the greatest value we provide our students in law school is often in the small-group and one-on-one work that we do. We cannot do that all the time, but we should dedicate ourselves to preserving and enriching those places where the "high touch" work happens most effectively. That part can be hard to replicate online. Fortunately, that makes it one of our greatest opportunities for strength in the future. And experiential learning, in clinics, full-simulation courses, labs, and externship opportunities monitored and supported by faculty, will be an important differentiator in the future. The law schools that get the balance between theory and application right, and can handle a more permeable wall between the institution and the outside world, will be stronger for having done so.

Further, all law schools need to enable a culture of measurement—not merely "teaching to the test" (i.e., the bar exam), but rather programmatic assessment that leads to cycles of continuous improvement across the law school. Indeed, a strong assessment program is an important part of the mission of any university today, including the law school. Such a program supports a culture of measurement but does not complete it. Perhaps most important when discussing assessment is the understanding that a well-designed assessment program leads to *deeper student engagement and thus deeper and more lasting learning.* This is the best foundation for a comprehensive assessment program, and once faculty understand this, they should embrace it rather than resist it.

A diverse culture is also mission critical. Just as with assessment, a more diverse learning environment leads to better learning outcomes for every student. We must never forget that we are preparing our students *for their future, not our past*, and they will live in a much more diverse world than we have even today. The very best way to prepare them for that is to create a world within the university and law school that reflects the world they will go into.

The future of teaching and learning will only be more complex and demanding than it already is. In such an environment teacher support is essential. While much of that happens at the unit level, there are things the university can do to support teachers in each school. Great teachers pour themselves out every quarter and every semester, so programs for teacher enrichment and renewal are essential. In this new hybrid world requiring greater learning outcomes, we will be asking more of our teachers, and so we must support their training and their renewal.

At its core, a university is about teaching and training a new generation of citizens. Teaching is—or certainly should be—a joyous activity. Every teacher can tell their own personal stories about the "light bulb" moments that students have had under their tutelage. When you ask a teacher to tap into those moments, their eyes start smiling. This is a form of alchemy, and we must remain mindful of not describing it so comprehensively that we kill it, or thinking we can dump it all online. Not everything can be measured perfectly or replicated digitally. But if we connect a culture of innovation to the joy that teachers feel when they achieve "flow" in their classrooms, we will have made our universities even more compelling places to work and learn. Those institutions that can do this will not just survive; they will thrive in the coming future of higher education.

The Bifurcated Status of Faculty

Sometimes because of university concerns, and sometimes because of law school concerns—and sometimes both—at most law schools we have a bifurcation of faculty, with some tenured or on tenure-track, and others with a lower status, such as a short or long-term contract. This can be unhealthy and create an "us" vs. "them" dynamic, when of course we are all equally engaged in the education of our students.

While it might be nice, in some quarters, to return to the day when tenure-track faculty were the only kind of faculty, and everyone else was staff (at least it was clear), the realities of legal practice in the twenty-first century requires a multi-modal approach to teaching our students. We absolutely need—and will always need as an essential foundation—respected scholars of the law who are able to analyze and study the law from a position of remove. Sometimes, those faculty members need to take unpopular and challenging positions, and tenure provides an important protection for them. And if they can also take controversial positions in the current life and development of the law, this is another important reason for the protections of tenure. If we undermine these foundational aspects of a law faculty, some of whom are protected by tenure, we risk no longer being able to consider what we are and do a law school.

But we are not just a law school. We are also a lawyer school. And so we also need law faculty who have made a long-term commitment to the institution and to their teaching who come from a different perspective and background, and who focus less on doctrinal development in the law and more on teaching the skills our students need to become the lawyers they came to us to become—and are making a tremendous financial investment in becoming.

When we think we are better than our peers, or write better scholarship, it might be helpful to be reminded of this truth, from Clay Shirkey, Vice Provost of Educational Technologies at New York University:

> Sometimes we try to make ourselves smarter. We call that research. Sometimes we try to make our peers smarter. We call that publishing. Sometimes we try to make our students smarter. We call that teaching. And that's it. That's all there is. These are important jobs for sure, and they are hard jobs at times, but they're not magic. And neither are we.[2]

The role of those who focus most of their efforts on scholarship is vital in every law school. The role of those who focus most of their efforts on teaching is also vital. Both need to be equally valued, and our faculties need to be integrated, not siloed from each other.[3]

---

2. Clay Shirkey, *Your Massively Open Offline College is Broken*, The Awl (February 7, 2013), https://www.theawl.com/2013/02/your-massively-open-offline-college-is-broken/.

3. Rachel Arnow-Richman, *Integrated Learning, Integrated Faculty*, 92 Temp. L. Rev. 745, 750 (2020).

The Buildings We Have

One of the issues we will have to face is that the law school buildings we have, many of which are fairly new in the last twenty-five years, were designed for the old model of delivering law school instruction. While online technology was available when these buildings were being built, they still were largely designed around large classrooms, where sixty to ninety students came together with the teacher at the same time. Large classes such as this were—all the way back to Langdell—always a financial decision, not a pedagogical one.

Imagining a building for the future of legal education is an interesting exercise. It would likely convert some of the larger classrooms into more modular rooms with movable tables and multiple screens around the room to support collaborative work among smaller groups of students. Not much work has been done on this in law schools yet, but it is an issue on the horizon, because the new model for legal education will have much less need for those large lecture halls.

A New Model for Legal Education

This book proposes a substantially revamped and redesigned curriculum for the three years of legal education. It proposes that we redesign the first year of law school to be in a hybrid online format, to a much larger cohort at substantially lower cost per student, and that we dispense with the LSAT and redesign the admissions process. After the hybrid first year, a test of substantive law and practical writing skills would be required to advance into second and third year, with those years in hybrid online and in-person format and substantially focused on experiential learning modalities.

One of the immediate concerns about a heavily online program during the first year is the traditional legal research and writing ("LRW") program, which in most schools is less content-based than the doctrinal courses and places a heavy emphasis on skills training and development. Some of the learning outcomes of LRW are harder to accomplish in a fully or heavily online program.[4] The answer to this concern is to provide an *Introduction* to Legal Writing I & II for one online credit each in the fall and spring of the first year. This

4. *See generally* David I. C. Thomson, *Effective Methods for Teaching Legal Writing Online* (Univ. of Denver Sturm Coll. of L. Legal Rsch. Paper Series, Working Paper No. 08-17, 2008) (discussing which LRW learning outcomes are difficult to replicate in an online program, and then suggesting remedies for these difficulties).

course then provides some legal writing experience that 1Ls need to effectively accomplish the first year essay examinations, but saves for the second year more in-person instruction in the traditional LRW pedagogy.

The *Carnegie Report* on legal education argued for the integration of law school instruction. Hybrid online instruction can do this more effectively than the traditional law school classroom because (to be successful) it requires a careful backward design of each course, which offers opportunities for integration. A curricular model for a redesigned program for legal education, which incorporates the principles of reducing cost and expanding experiential and integrated learning is presented in greater detail in Chapter Six.

We Must Dispense with the LSAT

As has been noted, law schools have struggled to enroll a sufficiently diverse class, one that reflects the general population and the applicant pool as a whole. This has been a perennial problem, but one that has been difficult to solve, and it has led to a less diverse profession that many would hope for and would be reasonable to expect.[5] The world our students are preparing to join will be even more diverse even than the one we have today (in all senses of that term)[6] and it is imperative that we provide a learning environment that is diverse and inclusive. But law students are accepted to law schools based primarily on their LSAT score (a standardized test that every applicant must take), and their undergraduate GPA. Because it has been shown that LSAT scores are disproportionately lower for many ethnic groups,[7] this has essentially acted as

5. *See, e.g.,* Deborah L. Rhode, *Law is the Least Diverse Profession in the Nation. And Lawyers Aren't Doing Enough to Change That*, Wash. Post (May 27, 2015), https://www.washingtonpost.com/posteverything/wp/2015/05/27/law-is-the-least-diverse-profession-in-the-nation-and-lawyers-arent-doing-enough-to-change-that/.

6. *See Nation Continues to Age as it Becomes More Diverse, U.S. Census Bureau* (June 30, 2022), https://www.census.gov/newsroom/press-releases/2022/population-estimates-characteristics.html (noting that the U.S. population is getting older and more diverse, indicating the United States is racially diversifying).

7. *See* Marjorie M. Shultz & Sheldon Zedeck, *Predicting Lawyer Effectiveness: Broadening the Basis for Law School Admission Decisions*, 36 L. & Soc. Inquiry 620, 621 (2011) ("Research consistently shows that affluent White students perform better on standardized tests, including the LSAT, than their less advantaged or minority peers."); William D. Henderson, *The LSAT, Law School Exams, and Meritocracy: The Surprising and Undertheorized Role of Test-Taking Speed*, 82 Tex. L. Rev. 975, 978, 982 (2004) (citing studies finding that historically, minority students have achieved "significantly lower scores than their white counterparts" and that time-limited tests have a disproportionate effect on performance of minority students).

a barrier to the kind of inclusive profession that many of us think we need to solve the legal problems of the twenty-first century.

Professor William Kidder examined this issue in his ground-breaking study of the subject.[8] He concluded that racial and ethnic gaps on the LSAT are larger than differences in undergraduate GPA, law school grades, or success in the legal profession.[9] His data resulted in the following findings within his sample group at Berkeley Law School:

1. African Americans scored on average 9.2 points lower on the LSAT than white students. This is greater than a standard deviation (of the national applicant pool).
2. Chicanos and Latinos scored on average 6.8 points lower.
3. Native Americans scored on average four points lower.

Ten years later, an additional study at Stanford confirmed Professor Kidder's findings. Professor Marjorie Shultz concluded that admission practices based upon standardized test admission (namely, the LSAT) reinforces racial and class privileges.[10] Her work also referenced Wightman, who concluded "that sole reliance on LSAT and UGPA would result in systematic exclusion of minorities from law school programs."[11] These tests are often looked at as a way to predict law school success, but while they are a moderate predictor of first year GPA, they do not correlate well to success in a law career.[12]

The ABA allowed the Graduate Record Examination (GRE) in 2016, and since then, over 70 law schools have announced that they would be accepting the GRE in lieu of the LSAT.[13] However, there are reasons to be concerned about the GRE as a predictor of law school performance—by minorities—as well.

In a study published in 1985, Professors Richard Scott and Marvin Shaw found that for both races studied, the GRE was a statistically good predictor

8. William C. Kidder, Comment, *Does the LSAT Mirror or Magnify Racial and Ethnic Differences in Educational Attainment? A Study of Equally Achieving "Elite" College Students*, 89 Calif. L. Rev. 1055, 1123 (2001).

9. *Id.* at 1074.

10. Kristen Holmquist et al., *Measuring Merit: The Shultz-Zedeck Research on Law School Admissions*, 63 J. Legal Educ. 565, 572–573 (2014).

11. Shultz & Zedeck, *supra* note 7, at 623.

12. *Id.*

13. *See, e.g.*, Alex Swoyer, *Top Law Schools Accepting GRE Instead of LSAT to Broaden Pool*, Wash. Times (Jan. 1, 2018), https://www.washingtontimes.com/news/2018/jan/1/gre-being-accepted-by-top-law-schools-instead-of-l/.

of GPA.[14] However, the relationship between GRE score and GPA was different for African-American and white students; for white students there was a positive corollary, whereas for African-American students there was a negative relationship—just the inverse.[15] Given this research, it is not clear that the GRE will be any more reliable as a predictor of performance in law school than the LSAT has been.

So, we must finally dispense with the LSAT and the GRE as a barrier, making law school more accessible for minority students in one stroke. Instead of being judged on their LSAT score—a test that has little relationship to what lawyers do[16]—students in the primarily online first year would be judged on how well they learned what lawyers need to know. If some students did not advance, they would have paid a lower cost for a basic understanding of how the law operates, which would be a public good in itself.[17] A master's degree in American law would be conferred, and it might be all those students want or need. Further, those 1L graduates could take a small amount of additional training and be ready to be a Limited License Legal Technician (LLLT). And those graduates could afford to do this, because their investment was so much less. Expansion of LLLTs will go a long way toward addressing the access to justice issue as well.

We Must Redesign the Admissions Process

If we abolish the LSAT as a barrier to admission to a revamped law school, we will need to come up with something else that satisfies our admissions professionals, not to mention the ABA. Fortunately, while this might require some additional staff in the admissions office, it should not be difficult to do. Indeed, much of the conceptual work has already been done.

---

14. Richard R. Scott & Marvin E. Shaw, *Black and White Performance in Graduate School and Policy Implications of the Use of Graduate Record Examination Scores in Admissions*, 54 J. Negro Educ. 14, 19 (1985).

15. *Id.*

16. Shultz & Zedeck, *supra* note 7, at 624–25 (citing a number of studies and reports identifying qualities that are at least as, if not more, predictive of professional success than the analytical reasoning skills measured by the LSAT). *See also* David L. Chambers et al., *Michigan's Minority Graduates in Practice: The River Runs Through Law School*, 25 L. & Soc. Inquiry 395, 401 (2000) ("LSAT scores . . . correlate with law school grades, but they seem to have no relationship to success after law school, whether success is measured by earned income, career satisfaction, or service contributions.").

17. For a more detailed explanation of the budgetary impact of this proposal, see Chapter Eight.

Traditionally, law school admissions have focused on finding students who are motivated to become a lawyer, and who can handle the work. The former is (generally) assessed from the prospective student's personal statement, and letters of recommendation. The latter is (generally) assessed from the prospective student's performance on the LSAT and their undergraduate GPA. Processing thousands of applications every year is already a difficult job, and law school admissions offices work hard to build a class every year. And they generally do build a class with those two criterion in mind. But this book suggests these are not the right criterion.

Instead, once we dispense with the LSAT, we only have undergraduate GPA to go on as an indicator if the student can handle the work required. Fortunately, that is sufficient, because the new model proposed here will admit a much larger cohort of students for a primarily online first year of law school, with a rigorous test at the end of the first year to either award the master's in American law to those who do not do sufficiently well (or decide to stop there), and graduate about roughly half of those students into the second year of law school.

The advantage of this approach is that we admit students to the rest of law school based on their *proven ability to do the work*, rather than a discriminatory instrument. This approach captures students who would not do well on the LSAT but it turns out do have a capacity to do the work required. If one accepts that the LSAT is a discriminatory instrument, it means some percentage of students who were rejected from law school actually *could* do the work, but the doors are closed to them.[18]

But the question of motivation to do the work is also an important one. And this can be determined in the ways it already has been—through a personal statement and letters of recommendation. Further, it could become the norm that applicants have worked for at least a year prior to applying to law school, as it has been in business school for decades. What is needed is a deeper examination of the motivation question—including from that gained by work experience—and this could be achieved through the activation of each school's alumni network. Many colleges do this—they have alumni from the college who live around the country conduct local interviews of prospective students and report back to the college their in-person impressions. Many medical schools do this as well. Law schools should also use a personal interview for all admissions.

---

18. Aaron N. Taylor, *The Marginalization of Aspiring Black Lawyers*, 13 FIU L. Rev. 489, 505–506 (2019).

And what would those alumni ask in those interviews? Beyond their motivation and desire to be a lawyer, one of the valuable avenues of inquiry should be informed by the Foundations for Practice study conducted by the Institute for the Advancement of the American Legal System (IAALS).[19] That study, of over 24,000 attorneys around the country about what they look for and need in a new lawyer to hire, found a broad and substantial requirement for what has been called "soft skills."

Among these are "work collaboratively as part of a team," "have passion for the work," "enjoy overcoming challenges," "seek and be responsive to feedback," "show integrity and trustworthiness," "have a commitment to justice and the rule of law," "react calmly and steadily in challenging and critical situations," and "exhibit resilience after a setback." A law school application process without a personal interview is less likely to be able to determine a prospective student's abilities in these areas. And if they do not have those qualities when they get to law school, they are unlikely to have a foundation upon which they will suddenly develop them during the three years, although intentional efforts to promote the formation of their professional identity can help, as discussed in Chapter Three.

As we admit a different cohort to law school, detailed assessment of their progress becomes even more important.

We Must Have a Culture of Measurement in Law Schools

There has been much discussion recently in legal education about the need for improvements in assessment. The American Bar Association has responded by adding an assessment requirement to the accreditation standards, making the subject even more urgent.[20] Because most of us in the legal academy are new to the language and methods of assessment there have been misunderstandings. And further, because there are different levels of assessment and

19. *Foundations for Practice: Survey Overview and Methodological Approach*, Inst.for the Advancement of the American Legal System, Univ. Denv., July 26, 2016, https://iaals.du.edu/publications/foundations-practice-survey-overview-and-methodological-approach.

20. The A.B.A. adopted Standards 301(b), 302, 314, and 315—all of which relate to assessment—in August 2014. They went into effect for students entering law school in the fall of 2016. Memorandum from Managing Director, A.B.A. Section of Legal Educ. and Admission to the Bar (June 2015) available at https://www.aals.org/wp-content/uploads/2015/06/ABA-Guidance-Stds-301-302-314-315-June-2015.pdf.

each level usually has different goals, sometimes the discussion can become confused.

Over the last few years many law school faculty have reacted to the increased focus on assessment in an understandable but dismissive way: "What? I know how to give my students a great final exam, and to grade them. I know all about assessment!" And some have felt threatened by the discussion, since they worry that this increased focus will challenge how they grade their students, and many believe in the accuracy of their methods. Worse, many also worry that this discussion is really a veiled attempt to violate their academic freedom and tell them what to teach.[21]

This difficult and at times confused discussion has been spurred primarily by two related developments. First, university-level accreditation bodies are focusing more on assessment and requiring the universities they accredit to have a well-designed assessment plan. Universities, in turn, are starting to require law schools to prepare assessment plans and submit them to a central assessment office for review. Second, the law school accreditation body—the American Bar Association—has recently moved towards requiring more assessment efforts in legal education. So, forces are converging on law schools requiring that they engage with this topic more deeply. Perhaps it is best to start with the ABA accreditation standard:

> Standard 314—Assessment of Student Learning
>
> A law school shall utilize both formative and summative assessment methods in its curriculum to measure and improve student learning and provide meaningful feedback to students.[22]

This requirement, taken alone, is unfortunately vague, and as a result, assessment plans in most law schools have so far been an insignificant affair. Of course, all law schools include both formative and summative assessment already, so it is not clear whether this standard is suggesting an adjustment,

---

21. Some faculty might also be concerned that if students are asked about outcomes in their end-of-semester evaluation of the course, such feedback might impact teaching assignments or contract renewals (for 405(c) faculty). Of course, it is hard to defend such a position; if a teacher says a learning outcome for a course is "X," and a student does not feel they learned that "X" material or skill in the course, they probably should be allowed to give such feedback to the teacher and the school.

22. A.B.A. Section of Legal Educ. & Admission to the Bar, Standards and Rules of Procedure for Approval of Law Schools 2022, Standard 314 (2022).

such as encouraging more formative assessment. All summative exams measure student learning, and an argument can be made that they improve student learning as well (students generally get better at taking them during law school)—is this suggesting that nothing needs to be done? Or will a midterm exam added to many (if not most) courses suffice to "provide meaningful feedback"? Worse, the two interpretations provided for Standard 314 are unhelpful as well. The first one explains the difference between summative assessments (such as final exams) and formative assessment (such as mid-semester feedback that students can use to improve their work in the course). The second one makes clear that the ABA was not asking schools to "apply multiple assessment methods" in any particular course, and that schools are not required to "use any particular assessment method."

Fortunately, the ABA did not stop there; Standard 315 and the interpretation that follows it provide more support for a substantial assessment process in law schools.

> Standard 315—Evaluation of Program of Legal Education, Learning Outcomes, and Assessment Methods
>
> The dean and the faculty of a law school shall conduct ongoing evaluation of the law school's program of legal education, learning outcomes, and assessment methods; and shall use the results of this evaluation to determine the degree of student attainment of competency in the learning outcomes and to make appropriate changes to improve the curriculum.[23]

The interpretation that follows this Standard supports a more robust assessment model in law school because it provides examples of methods that "may be used to measure the degree to which students have attained competency in the school's student learning outcomes...." Some of those methods are the traditional ones (bar exam passage rates, placement rates) but some are new, such as "student learning portfolios, and student performance in [courses] that...assess a variety of skills and knowledge."[24] This accreditation standard—taken together with the interpretation—sound more like what assessment is supposed to be about: not just final exams or even midterms in particular courses, but an evaluative process conducted across the curriculum

---

23. *Id.* at Standard 315.

24. *Id.* at Interpretation 315-1.

and throughout the law school. Unfortunately, it remains unclear whether the ABA is encouraging assessment that takes place at the school level (bar exam passage), the course level (student performance), the program level (learning portfolios), or all three.

Simplifying Assessment: It's a Process

Because of the lack of clarity in the new standards, a review of what the development of an assessment plan is supposed to entail might be helpful.[25] But first, one of the first things to understand about assessment is that it is not an event but rather a continual cyclical process. At its best, an assessment plan has a goal of continuous improvement, which operates through a repeating cycle. There are many explanations easily found on the web that illustrate assessment cycles, but the steps involved are essentially the same: (1) articulate measurable student learning outcomes, i.e., goals and objectives; (2) teach your students; (3) measure those outcomes; (4) make adjustments to what is being taught or assessed (or both) based on those measurements; and (5) rinse and repeat. Here is a simplified diagram of the cycle:

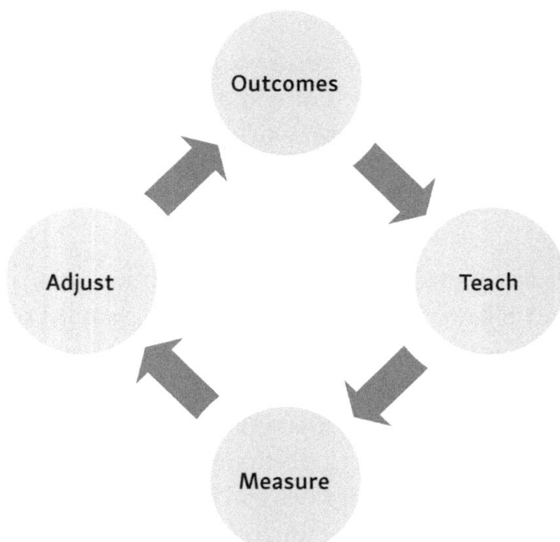

25. Portions of this chapter were first published in David I. C. Thomson, *When the ABA Comes Calling, Let's Speak the Same Language of Assessment*, 23 Perspectives: Teaching Legal Rsch. & Writing 68 (2014) and is reprinted here with permission.

First, a learning outcome is something you hope and plan for your students to be able to do with what you teach them over the course or a course segment. A *measurable* learning outcome is one that is, quite obviously, measurable, not merely aspirational. So, we want to set learning outcomes for our students that can be measured with a rubric or similar grading and review process based on work they have done during the course of the semester (and at the end of the semester). Second, it is important to tie the measurement you conduct of student work in the semester to the outcome you set. So, the professor should give some thought to whether the instrument of measurement (exam, oral presentation, written document) is designed to accurately measure student progress towards the learning goal that they set.

Third, if we engage in the first and second steps fully, we will usually discover that students are not learning all that we wanted them to learn, or not fully able to do what we hoped they could do. Ideally, this inquiry leads to a focus on making adjustments to the course materials or subjects addressed or teaching methodologies used (or some of each). Sometimes it leads to revisions to the learning outcomes—either because they were discovered to be less precise than we hoped, difficult to measure, or just do not reflect what we wanted our students to learn. So adjustments are made—either to the learning outcomes or to the measurement of those outcomes or to the teaching methods, or a combination of all of these. Note that it is important that a teacher be willing to make changes during a course—even midstream—to reflect weaknesses in their own teaching or their students' learning, but not to merely adjust outcomes to downgrade student expectations. An effective assessment plan is aimed at improving both teachers' teaching and learners' learning. Overall, the purpose of engaging in this methodology is that, ideally, it *all* gets better: continuous improvement throughout the law school.

When we encounter colleagues of good faith who find engaging in this process to be threatening, perhaps the best thing would be to respond with this question: "What could possibly be wrong with writing out a list of things you would like your students to know and be able to do at the end of the course or program you teach?" Most law school faculty, given a relatively short timeframe, could make that list with little difficulty. And then perhaps the follow up could be: "Having made that list, what could possibly be wrong with considering the best ways to measure achievement of those things you want your students to know or be able to do?" Often, the answer to these two inquiries is: "Actually, making the list wasn't difficult. And I think my final exam does a good job, or I can tell from the papers they write, that they did (or did not) achieve the goals that I have for them." Having gotten that far, usually faculty become engaged in the process of making adjustments when they feel their goals for their students are not being met. When it becomes part of the culture to do this on a regular basis, continuous improvement will be a natural by-product.

Having simplified the assessment process in this chapter, the reality is that the new ABA Standards will, over time, likely be more complex in application. Discussions about assessment can quickly become confused or confusing because it is not immediately clear what sort of assessment is involved, at what level the assessment is taking place, and/or what the goal of the assessment program is going to be. This is exacerbated by the indeterminate nature of the standards, which adds to the confusion. Because there are several different goals and levels of assessment, it is important that we understand those differing goals and levels so that when we speak of assessment to each other we are oriented to the sort of assessment effort we are talking about, and we can more immediately understand each other.

Assessment takes place (or should take place) at four different levels in law schools: (1) the student level, (2) the course level, (3) the program level, and (4) the school level. And there are two different goals to most assessment efforts: continuous improvement of student learning and providing affirming evidence of the value and efficacy of the educational opportunity being offered. These levels and goals—and their relationship to each other—can be illustrated in the diagram below:

Level	"Where we are now"	Goal: Continuous Improvement of Student Learning	Goal: Providing Evidence of Effective Instruction
Student	Mostly Summative Assessment	Formative Assessment	Students are learning what the course is designed to teach them
Course	Not often happening	Formative and Summative Assessment	The course is meeting its learning goals across the students enrolled
Program	Rare	Cross-Course, Program-wide Assessment	The Program is meeting its learning goals across classes and faculty members in the program
School	Bar Exam	School-wide assessment for curricular adjustments	The school is achieving school-wide learning outcomes

At the student level, the most common goal is to measure how much of a subject the student learned over the course of the semester. Traditionally, this has been done through a final exam, or what is known as summative assessment, where it is the sum of the learning that is assessed. As law school curricula move toward more skills courses and experiential learning, the preferred method of assessment is formative in nature—that is, the assessment helps to form the student's learning and to help them improve over the course of the semester.

At the course level, the most common goal is continuous improvement of student learning, both that year and in the future. Its simplest form is illustrated in the brief review of the assessment cycle, above. When measurable goals are articulated and measured throughout the course, improvements can be made to the course year over year. This refers to course level assessment—improving student learning in the course each year.

Program level assessment is something that is in its infancy in law schools but will likely be a part of most assessment plans going forward. The idea of program level assessment is to look at all similar courses, such as the legal writing program as a whole, or the clinic as a whole, or courses in a certificate program as a whole. This sounds difficult and complicated but does not have to be.[26] Such an assessment program may have as a goal continuous improvement of student learning in the program. But it may have a different aim as well: to assess how the entire program is achieving its learning goals *as a program*.[27]

School level assessment is the "Holy Grail" in law school assessment, and some would say just as unachievable. But this would involve an effort to set learning outcomes for the entire program of study, with either a goal of improvement of student learning or evidence of effective instruction.

For school level assessment with the second goal we have long had the bar exam. And indeed, we still do. More importantly, undergraduate education does not have anything similar, and neither does graduate business education. Accounting (for the CPA), medicine (for Board certification) and architecture

---

26. David I. C. Thomson, *Using Student Evaluation Data to Examine and Improve Your Program*, 21 Perspectives: Teaching Legal Rsch. & Writing 115 (2013).

27. Such a plan for programmatic assessment can be fraught with issues. Faculty are often understandably concerned that such a program-wide assessment effort might be a veiled attempt to ferret out particularly poor-performing teachers. But that is for the review process, and as long as anonymity by professor can be maintained in the data collection process and its review, it should be workable for all concerned.

(for the ARE designation) have similar requirements. So from an assessment officer's point of view, having the bar exam seems like a plus.

But the unfortunate reality is that the bar exam is not a proper assessment tool for school-wide success in preparing its graduates for practice, and it has its own discriminatory impacts. It does, of course, test knowledge and skills—on a clock—that are used and needed in practice. But the mere fact that the bar exam was never developed in conjunction with a school-wide, legal education-wide, cyclical assessment effort indicates that it is not a proper assessment instrument. At the school level, however, it is all we have.

There is one exception, and it is a bright spot in legal education. It is the Daniel Webster Scholars Honors Program at the University of New Hampshire.[28] This program was developed specifically to prepare its graduates for practice in New Hampshire, and indeed when they graduate from the program, they are admitted to the New Hampshire Bar without taking a bar exam. This is because the program was designed with assessment in mind, and numerous formative and summative assessments have taken place over the course of the three-year program so that the need for a bar exam is eliminated.

Multiple Choice Tests Are Not Formative Assessment

In the developing discussions around law school assessment, some professors have asked whether it is possible for multiple-choice tests to be formative assessment. If it were, then the addition of formative assessment to the standards would be a fairly easy element to add to the curriculum.

The core difference between summative and formative assessment can be explained this way: formative assessments are designed primarily to *improve* learning, while summative assessments are designed primarily to *judge* learning.[29]

An essential feature of formative assessment is individualized feedback provided by the teacher beyond merely a test score that measures how far the student fell short of a set arbitrary standard. The feedback provided should detail what good performance looks like and explain why it is better than what the student did. Such feedback provides tools to the student that help them self-assess going forward and has been found to foster higher levels of engagement and motivation in learning the material.

---

28. For more information about the Daniel Webster Scholar Honors Program, see https://law.unh.edu/academics/daniel-webster-scholar-honors-program.

29. Jeanette Buttrey et al., *Using Case-Progression Approach to Mapping Learning Outcomes and Developing Assessments*, 95 U. Det. Mercy L. Rev. 283, 285–87 (2018).

Formative assessment should be designed to monitor student learning during the course, but also to allow the teacher to monitor and modify his or her teaching practices during the pendency of course. So there is an element of formation for the teacher as well as the student.

These definitions may be somewhat helpful, but perhaps a couple of examples might help to put the definitions in the context of law school teaching. A hypothetical law professor teaches an upper-level large course to sixty-five students and the professor gives a midterm that is mostly short and long answer essay format. There is a great deal of feedback given on each exam, together with a grade, which amounts to a quarter of the grade for the course. Then, the professor invites each student to appeal their grade, a challenge that many accept. The appeal must be in a prescribed written format, and the professor reviews each appeal and then meets with each student to give them the result of their appeal and explain it. This is the best of what we mean (in legal education) by formative assessment.

In contrast, another hypothetical law professor offers an exercise in first year contracts in which they have students prepare multiple choice questions (and proposed answers) for an optional test, and submit them in advance of the test, which uses versions of those questions (after an edit). This is certainly an interesting exercise, and probably fun for the students. But it is not clear what formative learning the students get from the professor in that exercise (other than from their question appearing on the optional test with or without modification). And it is not clear how the professor uses this exercise for their own learning and adjustment of the course while they are teaching it. So, this example does not have either of the two essential hallmarks of being a formative exercise.

Here is an illustration of a multiple-choice test that is not formative: take a hypothetical law professor who teaches a certain standard 1L course. That professor gives a multiple-choice midterm in the course and provides only scores to the students. Further, the content in the midterm is no longer addressed or used the rest of the semester, including on the final exam. So, this "midterm" is really a summative exam for a portion of the course, and it has very little formative value for the student. The student could get the same benefit on their own using a CALI lesson.[30]

30. The Center for Computer-Assisted Legal Instruction (CALI) provides and maintains over 1,000 online assessments for nearly every law school subject. For more information, *see*, http://www.cali.org.

Multiple-choice questions can be formative, but they should accomplish more than merely to judge the level of learning that has been accomplished. For example, when a multiple-choice test provides the student after the test with detailed explanations for the correct answers (as well as the incorrect answers), it can provide some guidance for improvement of comprehension of course content. But—particularly when testing skills—multiple-choice questions are most effectively formative when there is some individualized feedback provided by the professor to the student, *and* the professor uses the information gleaned from the assessment to adjust the teaching and learning activities in the course, ideally while the course is still underway.

Whether multiple-choice tests can be formative assessment (or not) is not a bright-line test, but the answer is generally no—at least not the way multiple-choice tests are most commonly used. However, a multiple-choice test *can* do these sorts of "formative" things for a student.

A score on a multiple-choice test can give the student a sense of how they are doing in retaining substantive knowledge, and depending on the question and its form, perhaps even how they are doing in developing a skill (such as legal analysis and application.)

If, when the score is received, a list of the correct answers is also provided, together with a description of why a certain question is correct, and why others are wrong, this can also be formative of learning for the student. But at the course level, to be formative, such tests have to be conducted during the course (such as a midterm) so the student has an opportunity to improve their understanding before the summative (final) exam.

If all that is being taught in the typical law school classroom is content, then perhaps several low stakes multiple-choice tests, with correct answer explanations provided afterwards, can fit that definition. And of course, if faculty are using such tests to identify where students are struggling—in content and skills—so they can address problems immediately in the course, well, that's further evidence that the purpose of the test was formative, for the student *and* the teacher.

But, of course, that is not all that is taught in the typical law school classroom. The much harder thing to reveal in a multiple-choice test is places where the critical "thinking and linking" is missing or off. Multiple-choice questions are not good at this (particularly ones developed generically by vendors rather than individual teachers for their own students), and the great temptation is to think they are, and skip over the intended benefits of formative assessment for learning and continuous improvement.

So, the term "formative assessment" refers to something deeper and more individualized—in its best form—than the sorts of things that multiple choice questions can do for students. Its most important and effective use is in providing qualitative feedback—as opposed to just scores—that is focused on the details of the performance with tailored guidance for each student on how to improve.

Finally, an important purpose of formative assessment is for the *teacher*, who uses evidence of student achievement to make adjustments to the course and methods of instruction, thus creating and contributing to a cycle of continuous improvement.

Conclusion

The old model for legal education, which dates back over 130 years, is—in some significant ways—outmoded for the 21st century, and for the practice lives that graduates will lead. This book offers a new, updated model that involves redesigning the first year of law school to put most of it into a hybrid online format, and to remove the LSAT as a barrier to entry, opening up the new first year to a larger cohort of students at lower cost. We also need to give greater emphasis to the formation of professional identity of our students and continue the process of gradually converting many of the upper-level credits to experiential learning formats.

As law schools continue to address the ABA requirement that they develop assessment plans, we need to create a culture of assessment across the board in legal education. And as we do so, we would all do well to understand what part of an assessment effort we are working on. It is essential that we are clear about what the goal of the assessment effort is, and what level of assessment we are focusing on, so that we can share information and learn from each other more efficiently about what we are doing and what is working as we move forward into the brave new world of law school assessment plans. Doing so is an essential component of the way forward.

THREE

We Must Integrate the Formation of Professional Identity

Introduction

In its landmark 2007 report on legal education, the Carnegie Foundation for the Advancement of Teaching focused its strongest criticism on the conclusion that law schools were not paying sufficient attention to the formation of professional identity in their students.[1] This was a relatively new concept to legal educators, although one they may have addressed occasionally in some courses and clinical offerings.[2] But the *Carnegie Report* put a spotlight on the obligation as follows:

> Because it always involves social relationships with consequences, [law] practice ultimately depends on serious engagement with the meaning of the activities—in other words, with their moral bearing. For professionals, the decisive dimension is responsibility for clients and for the values the public has entrusted to the profession.[3]

This chapter offers a framework for addressing this need in the law curriculum of the future. It is particularly important now, as the ABA has added a requirement to the accreditation standards that law schools "shall provide

1. *See* Carnegie Report, *supra* ch.1, note 12, at 14.
2. *See id.* at 12–14.
3. *Id.* at 11–12.

substantial opportunities to students for the development of professional identity."[4]

It is instructive to remember that the *Carnegie Report* was part of a series of reports on education for the professions and included reports on the training of doctors, nurses, clergy, and engineers.[5] In each report, Carnegie Foundation authors emphasized the professional formation of the student.[6] However, perhaps because the legal profession already had a code of professional conduct[7] and the ABA already required every law school to teach professional ethical rules,[8] many legal educators did not understand what exactly was missing. As a result of the report encouraging the emphasis of professional identity formation in a curriculum that already had a required course dedicated to ethics, there was confusion. It did not help that the report unintentionally blurred the distinction between the required course in ethics (and its emphasis on the ethical rules) that has long been a part of legal education and the new concept introduced in the report: the *formation of professional identity*.[9] It took legal educators some time to realize that buried in the report was a concept that was almost completely new to them. Many had little idea what it was, reduced as it was in their minds to the concept of *professionalism*; and, having scant understanding that it was something different, had done very little to address it in legal education. This chapter offers a definition of professional identity for lawyers, starting with what a profession is, and how that term applies to the legal profession.[10]

The concept of a "profession" started with medicine and dates back to the fifth century B.C.[11] The medical profession was the first to combine prom-

---

4. A.B.A. Accreditation Standards, Standard 303(b)(3).

5. Carnegie Report, *supra* ch. 1, note 12, at 15.

6. *See* Anne Colby & William M. Sullivan, *Formation of Professionalism and Purpose: Perspectives from the Preparation for the Professions Program*, 5 U. St. Thomas L.J. 404, 405, 410 (2008).

7. *See* Model Rules of Prof'l Conduct pmbl. para. 7 (2013).

8. *See* A.B.A. Section of Legal Educ. and Admission to the Bar, A.B.A. Standards and Rules of Procedure for Approval of Law Schools 2014–2015, Standard 303(a)(1) (2014) [hereinafter A.B.A. Standards 2014–2015].

9. *See* Carnegie Report, *supra* note 1, at 129.

10. Portions of this chapter were originally published in: David I. C. Thomson, *"Teaching" Formation of Professional Identity*, 27 Regent U. L. Rev. 303 (2014–15) and is reprinted here with permission.

11. *See* Steven H. Miles, The Hippocratic Oath and the Ethics of Medicine (Oxford Univ. Press 2004). The Hippocratic Oath is an early embodiment of the concept of a profession. *Id.* at 3.

ises of scientific expertise with individual moral commitments.[12] Interestingly (and appropriately, given how little about the human body was known), among those moral commitments were humility and a promise to learn from one's and others' mistakes.[13] Even to the present day, the core of medical professional identity is found in what is known as the Hippocratic Oath, and most students recite the oath upon graduation from medical school.[14]

The root word of professional is *profess*, or to declare something in public.[15] The dictionary definition of that word is: "to declare or admit openly or freely: affirm."[16] A group of people who declare principles to which they will adhere constitutes a profession, and each professional thereby limits his options and behaves in conformance with the declared set of values. Lawyers, of course, declare openly that they will adhere to the Rules of Professional Conduct, the ethical standards of the legal profession.[17] Roscoe Pound defined a profession as a group "pursuing a learned art as a common calling in the spirit of a public service—no less a public service because it may incidentally be a means of livelihood."[18] So lawyering is done as a "common calling"—we do it in common, and we are "called" to work in "the spirit of public service." The question then becomes: What are the standards for moral behavior in service to the public for lawyers? Is it simply the ethical standards we have, or is it something more? And if it is something more, what does that mean for us as legal educators? Formal legal education has been criticized for being disconnected from the profession nearly since its inception, and a brief study of the more recent criticism might help to answer those questions.

---

12. *Id.*

13. *See id.* at xiii–xiv (binding the physician to use his ability and judgment to keep patients from harm or injustice and guard life in a pure and holy way).

14. Raphael Hulkower, *The History of the Hippocratic Oath: Outdated, Inauthentic, and Yet Still Relevant*, 25/26 Einstein J. Biology & Med. 41, 41 (2010).

15. Merriam-Webster's Collegiate Dictionary 928 (10th ed. 2001).

16. *Id.*

17. *See* Model Rules of Prof'l Conduct pmbl. (2013). The A.B.A. requires law schools to teach students these standards, and many lawyers swear an oath when admitted to the bar. *See id.* A.B.A. Standards 2014–2015, *supra* note 7; Carol Rice Andrews, *The Lawyer's Oath: Both Ancient and Modern*, 22 Geo. J. Legal Ethics 3, 44–57 (2009).

18. Roscoe Pound, The Lawyer from Antiquity to Modern Times 5 (1953). *See also*, Alan Paterson, Lawyers and the Public Good: Democracy in Action? 14–15 (Cambridge 2012).

What Is Formation of Professional Identity?

As we develop our thinking about professional identity formation we should be explicit about what it means. Since the *Carnegie Report* was published, the terms "professionalism" and "professional identity" have been confused with each other, and yet, they are mostly different concepts.[19] While there is some overlap between them, each contains components that are distinct from the other. The *Carnegie Report* uses this language to describe professional identity formation: "Th[e] apprenticeship of professional identity . . . include[s] conceptions of the personal meaning that legal work has for practicing attorneys and their sense of responsibility toward the profession."[20]

Thus, the original idea in the *Carnegie Report* included concepts of "personal meaning" and "responsibility." Further, the report argued that learning how to balance the competing interests in legal representation was critical to our students' formation:

> [L]egal education needs to attend very seriously to its apprenticeship of professional identity. . . . [S]tudents' great need is to begin to develop the knowledge and abilities that can enable them to understand and manage these tensions in ways that will sustain their professional commitment and personal integrity over the course of their careers.[21]

As a way of underscoring this important subject, the report argued that it was one with far-reaching consequences:

> Insofar as law schools choose not to place ethical-social values within the inner circle of their highest esteem and most central preoccupation, and insofar as they fail to make systematic efforts to educate toward a central moral tradition of lawyering, legal education may inadvertently

---

19. *Compare* Martin J. Katz, *Teaching Professional Identity in Law School*, 42 Colo. Law. 45, 45 (2013) (explaining that professional identity includes "more than simply ethics or professionalism—or even both together"), *with* Donald Burnett, *A Pathway of Professionalism—The First Day of Law School at the University of Idaho*, 52(2) Advocate 17, 18 (2009) (using the words "professional identity" and "professionalism" synonymously).

20. Carnegie Report, *supra* ch.1, note 12, at 132.

21. *Id.* at 128.

> contribute to the demoralization of the legal profession and its loss of a moral compass. . . .[22]

Having examined the *Carnegie Report* closely, we know that the concepts behind the third apprenticeship include personal meaning in the work, responsibility to the profession and society, and personal integrity.[23] Unfortunately, while introducing a potentially quite valuable concept into legal education, the *Carnegie Report* also adds some confusion to the difference between this new concept and the traditional concept of professional ethics as studied in law school.[24]

Part of this confusion comes simply through the various terms the report uses for the third apprenticeship. Chapter Four of the report is focused on this subject, and there are references to the "[a]pprenticeship of [i]dentity and [p]urpose," the "apprenticeship of professional identity," the "apprenticeship of professionalism and purpose," and the "ethical-social apprenticeship."[25] Further, there is confusion between the terms "professionalism" and "professional identity."[26] Is professional identity formation simply the same as professionalism? Or does it merely refer to the identity of being a professional attorney?

The *Carnegie Report*, offers this further prescription:

> Law school graduates who enter legal practice also need the capacity to recognize the ethical questions their cases raise, even when those questions are obscured by other issues and therefore not particularly salient. They need wise judgment when values conflict, as well as the integrity to keep self-interest from clouding their judgment.[27]

Some key terms in this prescription are worth highlighting: "ethical questions their cases raise," "wise judgment when values conflict," and "integrity to keep self-interest from clouding their judgment."[28]

---

22. *Id.* at 140.
23. Carnegie Report, *supra* ch.1, note 12, at 132.
24. *See* sources cited *supra* note 19.
25. Carnegie Report, *supra* ch.1, note 12, at 132.
26. *See* sources cited *supra* note 19.
27. Carnegie Report, *supra* ch.1, note 12, at 146.
28. *Id.*

It is possible for all these competing views and definitions to be reconciled. Doing so, however, will require that we separate the terms "professionalism" and "professional identity." It is important that we do this because, while the ethical rules include value judgments,[29] they are rules, and as such, are amenable to bad lawyering.[30] The values of the profession, however, are not fully contained in the ethical rules, and where they are addressed, they often reflect historical values that may be antiquated or include some undesirable values the profession ought to rethink.[31] Those values may be difficult to agree on, but that does not mean it is impossible or unrealistic to expect the profession to do so.[32] The *Carnegie Report* suggests that even though we have ethical rules that govern our behaviors, something is still missing, or at least sufficient focus on that something has been lost.[33]

While there is some overlap existing between the two concepts, these concepts are separable, and there is value in articulating two separate definitions and goals in this work and in our teaching. For these reasons, this chapter offers the following definition of what "professionalism" means to attorneys:

> Professionalism relates to the ethical rules (the line below which we cannot stray) as well as behaviors, such as thoroughness, respect and consideration for one's clients and towards opposing counsel and judges and responding to client needs in a timely fashion.

As we know, the *Carnegie Report* suggests that law schools are not giving sufficient attention to the formation of professional identity in law school.[34] But it could not have been referring to the concepts included in this definition of professionalism; we teach these concepts well in law school, not only in

---

29. *See* Andrew B. Ayers, *What If Legal Ethics Can't Be Reduced to a Maxim?*, 26 Geo. J. Legal Ethics 1, 2 (2013).

30. *See* W. Bradley Wendel, *Should Law Schools Teach Professional Duties, Professional Virtues, or Something Else? A Critique of the Carnegie Report on Educating Lawyers*, 9 U. St. Thomas L.J. 497, 518 (describing the Holmesian bad man approach to legal ethics).

31. *See* Eli Wald, *Resizing the Rules of Professional Conduct*, 27 Geo. J. Legal Ethics 227, 256 (2014) (explaining that the underlying assumptions of the Model Rules of Professional Conduct are inconsistent with the profession as a whole).

32. *See* David Luban, *How Must a Lawyer Be? A Response to Wooley and Wendel*, 23 Geo. J. Legal Ethics 1011, 1102 (2010) (arguing that mere difficulty is an insufficient reason to reject the conception of "moral agency").

33. *See* Carnegie Report, *supra* ch.1, note 12, at 127.

34. *See id.*

the ethics course, but also across the curriculum. Arguably, we could be more intentional about how and when we do this, but throughout the curriculum, beyond the required ethics course, we expect certain behaviors from our students. Often we define them in our course policy documents, and certainly they are defined in our student handbooks and honor codes.[35] We expect certain behaviors, and for the most part we get them. We could doubtless do a better job of engendering consideration for diverse clients and diverse client perspectives, but this is becoming a more intentional part of clinical pedagogy, as well as all forms of experiential learning.[36]

If that is an acceptable definition of professionalism, what is the *Carnegie Report* referring to when it argues in favor of law schools being more intentional about the work they do with their students in helping them to form a professional identity?

This chapter offers the following definition of what the *Carnegie Report* means when it describes the third apprenticeship:

> Professional identity relates to one's own decisions about professional behaviors "above the line," as well as a sense of duty as an officer of the legal system and responsibility as part of a system in our society that is engaged in preserving, maintaining, and upholding the rule of law.

The reason for the "above the line" distinction in this definition is this: no one goes to law school to learn how to violate the ethical rules.[37] Students want to know what is expected of them as professionals.[38] And not

---

35. *See generally, e.g.*, Academic Honor Code, Berkeley L., http://www.law.berkeley.edu/819.htm (last visited Mar. 10, 2015); Honor Code, Stan. Univ., https://studentaffairs.stanford.edu/communitystandards/policy/honor-code (last visited Mar. 10, 2015).

36. *See* Mary Lynch, *The Importance of Experiential Learning for Development of Essential Skills in Cross-Cultural and Intercultural Effectiveness*, 1 J. Experiential Learning 129, 131–32 (2015). It is now also a requirement under A.B.A. Standard 303(c).

37. No rational student would spend the tuition and attendant costs to attend law school just to run the risk of being disbarred and losing all of that investment.

38. *See* Helia Garrido Hull, *Legal Ethics for the Millennials: Avoiding the Compromise of Integrity*, 80 UMKC L. Rev. 271, 272–73 (2011) (noting stories of lawyers facing discipline or disbarment for lack of professionalism); Sabrina C. Narain, *A Failure to Instill Realistic Ethical Values in New Lawyers: The ABA and Law School's Duty to Better Prepare Lawyers for Real Life Practice*, 41 W. St. U. L. Rev. 411, 415–16 (2014) (noting that most professional responsibility courses focus on the "basic framework to avoid malpractice liability and disciplinary actions by the state bar").

all situations—indeed precious few of them in day-to-day practice—require that the attorney take a position that is *right on the ethical line*.[39] So professional identity must involve personal decisions of where the attorney will apply judgment to decide how to resolve particular ethical matters that reside "above the line."[40] Such decisions importantly involve both matters of morality and matters of identity.

And so then the concept of *teaching* professional identity means we want our students to experience making these sorts of decisions while they are still in law school so they have some idea of how they would resolve them when they arise in practice. When we say we "teach" professional identity, it means we ask our students to finish this sentence: "I am a *lawyer*, and that means for *me* that *I* will resolve this *above the line* ethical dilemma as follows. . . ." The *Carnegie Report* is probably correct when it says most law schools do not *teach* that—or when they do, not intentionally or very well—across the curriculum.[41]

Yes, This Can and Must Be "Taught"

With the emerging consensus that these are things we should teach our students comes the companion view that this is something we *can* teach. Indeed, "[t]he predominant view among legal educators is no longer that students can learn professional values by osmosis or on the job training. We have to teach it in law school."[42] A panel at the annual conference of the Association of American Law Schools (AALS) was entitled "Incorporating Teaching Pro-

39. *See* Luban, *supra* note 32, at 1116 ("By and large, lawyers do not go frantically through life encountering one moral dilemma after another like challenges in a video game.").

40. Because this part of the definition incorporates the ethical rules, it is the place of overlap between the two concepts of "professionalism" and "professional identity." *See* sources cited *supra* note 18.

41. Carnegie Report, *supra* ch.1, note 12, at 14, 146–47. For an early example of a legal ethics course that sought to teach formation, *see* William M. Sullivan & Matthew Rosen, A New Agenda for Higher Education 56–59 (Carnegie Foundation, 2008) (describing a course designed by Daisy Hurst Floyd at Mercer University Law School entitled *Advanced Legal Ethics: Finding Joy and Satisfaction in Legal Life*.)

42. Alison Donahue Kehner & Mary Ann Robinson, *Mission: Impossible, Mission: Accomplished or Mission: Underway? A Survey and Analysis of Current Trends in Professionalism Education in American Law Schools*, 38 U. Dayton L. Rev. 57, 99 (2012).

fessional Identity into the Legal Education Curriculum."[43] Law professors are a confident and hard-working bunch, and there is a broad assumption that this is something we can teach.

The problem for us as teachers is that formation of a student's identity is not directly "teachable," at least not in the didactic sense. As we have seen, professional formation in law happens in the context of work that is important for the welfare of society, and it involves judgment and concepts of one's personal identity as a human being and as a citizen and member of that society.[44] Because the subject is so personal to each student, the answers to such questions as "What do I really believe in?" and "What kind of a person do I want to be?" and, gradually, "What kind of a lawyer do I want to be?" are not something we can "teach," at least not through the methods common to law school classrooms.[45] We cannot effectively teach someone to answer such questions in the abstract. When we try to do that, we usually receive tentative answers disconnected from the legal context that animates them. The context and the value judgments students make are the bases from which they will form their professional identity as lawyers.[46]

We must also remember that all students come to law school with different backgrounds and educational experiences, all of which have formed them as human beings. Instead of thinking that ethical formation is something we can offer our students didactically—*teaching* in the standing-behind-the-podium sense—law faculty need to do something else. We need a pedagogical method by which we might address the third apprenticeship throughout the curricu-

43. Final Program at Association of American Law Schools 2015 Annual Meeting: Legal Education at the Crossroads 10 (Jan. 2–5, 2015) available at https://www.aals.org/wp-content/uploads/2014/12/Program_Final.pdf.

44. Nelson P. Miller, *An Apprenticeship of Professional Identity: A Paradigm for Educating Lawyers*, 87 Mich. Bar J. 20, 23 (2008) (noting that part of professionalism training must include the concept of a lawyer as a citizen of the United States).

45. *See* Kathleen Clark, *The Legacy of Watergate for Legal Ethics Instruction,* 51 Hastings L.J. 673, 676 (2000) ("[A] student needs to engage not just her intellect, as she might in puzzling out the intricacies of federal jurisdiction, but she must also engage her heart, to determine how she will feel in a professional situation she may face.").

46. It should be noted, of course, that clinical and externship faculty have often worked on these matters more intentionally than other parts of the typical law school faculty. However, the goal of this chapter is also to be helpful in clinic and externship programs, since the framework provided here could also provide guidance in those contexts.

lum.[47] It is likely this will be something different than the familiar one-to-many classroom framework in which we are most comfortable.

More than fifteen years after the publication of the *Carnegie Report*, few schools are engaged in intentional professional identity formation, and those that are rarely have a program that addresses all of its students. An ABA Curricular Survey indicates that where such opportunities have been made available, they are mostly in upper-level electives.[48] In another study of the professionalism-related course offerings in American law schools, the authors found that professionalism instruction exists (however that might be defined by the survey respondent) in only 16 percent of doctrinal courses.[49] With the new ABA requirement that schools provide "substantial opportunities" to students for the development of their professional identity, this will need to change.

Unfortunately, there are significant limitations to the current attempts to teach formation of professional identity, however well-designed and intentioned they may be. Because the nature of professional formation is interwoven with personal formation, these specialized courses by nature must be small. The first year courses are difficult to implement across the first year class, and where they have been implemented, they required a broad institutional commitment to the work; indeed, it became integrated into the school's culture—no easy task to achieve.[50] First year students are also being pushed and pulled in many different directions in their other courses, and that makes it a difficult season to devote so much time to these concepts.

More concerning, however, is that even though these courses use problems set in the context of practice, they are non-contextual for all students. So much of professional formation is localized in the area of practice of the graduate. Another worry is that such courses could allow the remainder of the faculty—those who are not engaged in these forms of education—to think that it is being taken care of elsewhere. But of course, the *Carnegie Report*'s most

47. Denise Platfoot Lacey, *Embedding Professionalism into Legal Education*, 18 J.L. Bus. & Ethics 41, 46 (2012).

48. *See* Catherine L. Carpenter, *A Survey of Law School Curricula: 2002–2010* (ABA 2012) [hereinafter *2002–2010 A.B.A. Curricular Survey*].

49. Kehner & Robinson, *supra* note 42, at 85–86.

50. *See, e.g.*, Neil Hamilton et al., *Empirical Evidence That Legal Education Can Foster Student Professionalism/Professional Formation to Become an Effective Lawyer*, 10 U. St. Thomas L.J. 11, 29 ("[F]aculty members . . . create[d] a curriculum and a culture in which each student can develop the knowledge and skills essential to becoming an excellent lawyer while also forming an ethical professional identity integrated with the student's faith and moral compass.").

fundamental recommendation was that the third apprenticeship be integrated throughout the curriculum.[51]

Indeed, perhaps the greatest concern about these efforts is that they are piecemeal—they do not ultimately achieve the goal of integration of the three apprenticeships across the curriculum. Professional formation not only needs to be contextual, but it also needs to be regular and repeated. As William Sullivan has written, "[m]ost importantly, when ethical professional practices and standards are enacted over and over in the course of training, students develop habits of heart and mind that shape their approach to their work for years to come."[52]

The nature of identity itself requires regular and repeated formation opportunities. Carrie Yang Costello is a sociologist who had prior training and practice experience as a lawyer, and she has written a book about professional identity formation in training for two professions (social work and law). In her book, Professor Costello notes that "our identities are like icebergs. The large bulk of them lies invisible to us below the surface of consciousness, while only a small part of them are perceptible to our conscious minds."[53] The non-conscious bulk of identity is referred to by sociologists as "habitus."[54] This includes taste, body language, and emotional identity.[55] When one's habitus is in dissonance with the professional identity of one's chosen profession, this leads in most cases to difficulty having success in the profession or added physical stress—and often both.[56] Only through repeated efforts to reconcile the two—or through finding a sub-specialty in the law that fits one's personal identity better than most others and working to reconcile that—is one likely to reduce the dissonance between one's identity and one's profession. It is there-

---

51. Carnegie Report, *supra* ch. 1, note 12 at 147.

52. Colby & Sullivan, *supra* note 6, at 421; *see also* Carnegie Report, *supra* ch. 1, note 12, at 191–92 (noting that the three apprenticeships—the cognitive, the practical, and the ethical-social—should be consistently integrated in law school curricula).

53. Carrie Yang Costello, Professional Identity Crisis: Race, Class, Gender, and Success at Professional Schools 20 (Vanderbilt Univ. Press 2005). Personal identity has been defined as "a person's deeply felt convictions about who she is, and what matters most to her existence as a worker, a citizen, and a human being." Howard Gardner et al., Good Work: When Excellence and Ethics Meet 11 (Basic Books 2002).

54. *Id*

55. *Id.* at 20–22.

56. *See id.* at 23.

fore important to "consistently emphasize the development of professional identity and purpose throughout."[57]

It is worth noting that law schools with a religious affiliation may have a head start in efforts to promote the formation of professional identity.[58] The University of St. Thomas School of Law is the home of the Holloran Center for Ethical Leadership in the Professions.[59] The school and center, within a Catholic university, have been leaders in developing courses and teaching methodologies for professional formation.[60] And Regent University School of Law, host of a symposium on professional identity, is part of a faith-based university that provides an education "rooted in a Christian perspective."[61] At these schools, discussions around faith and morality are connected to their missions and are a part of their cultures.[62] To a large extent, their students self-select to these institutions because they already have a personal identity that is formed, at least in part, by the belief system that is consonant with the school's mission.[63] At law schools without such a foundation or culture, pro-

---

57. Colby & Sullivan, *supra* note 6, at 423.

58. Jeffrey A. Brauch, *Faith-Based Law Schools and an Apprenticeship in Professional Identity*, 42 U. Tol. L. Rev. 593, 598 (2011) ("Faith-based law schools are well-positioned to provide the professional identity training that Carnegie finds generally lacking in legal education today.").

59. *See* Holloran Center for Ethical Leadership Profs., http://www.stthomas.edu/hollorancenter/ (last visited Mar. 11, 2015).

60. *Id.*; *The Vision of a Catholic College in the Midwest*, Univ. St. Thomas, http://www.stthomas.edu/aboutust/mission/ (last visited Mar. 11, 2015).

61. *Regent University Law Review Symposium Schedule*, Regent Univ. Sch. L., http://www.regent.edu/acad/schlaw/student_life/studentorgs/lawreview/symposiumschedule.cfm (listing the events for a legal symposium titled "Raising the Bar: How Developing a Professional Identity Can Help You Break the Negative Lawyer Stereotype") (last visited Mar. 11, 2015); *Why Regent*, Regent Univ., http://success.regent.edu/index.php (last visited Mar. 11, 2015).

62. Brauch, *supra* note 58, at 602 (noting that, at Regent University School of Law, professional identity is a focus both inside and outside the classroom).

63. *E.g.*, *Testimonials*, Ctr. for Ethical Formation and Legal Educ. Reform, http://www.regent.edu/acad/schlaw/programs/cef/testimonials.cfm (last visited Mar. 11, 2015) ("I knew that Regent was going to not only equip me academically and professionally, but it is also supportive of my values, viewing law as a means [of] glorifying God with our talents and knowledge."); *see also The Regent Law Difference*, Regent Univ. Sch. L., http://www.regent.edu/acad/schlaw/whyregentlaw/whyregentlaw.cfm (last visited Mar. 11, 2015) (recruiting students interested in legal education based on "eternal principles of truth and justice [that] inform the way we should teach, study, and practice law").

fessional formation discussions are more likely to be met with skepticism.[64] In the Carnegie Foundation's study of clergy education, it was noted that "[m]any theological schools are more self-conscious about their reliance on the forma-tive influences of the school's cultural practices. . . . [F]ormative communities of practice [are] a central mechanism of the third apprenticeship in theological education."[65] "Unfortunately," William Sullivan has noted, "the kind of inten-tionality with regard to campus culture as a formative mechanism that we see in clergy education is rare in most other professional schools."[66]

Teaching Simulations Supports Formation

What is becoming clear is that we need to not simply lecture about profes-sional formation, but instead create realistic "situations" in which our students can be confronted with ethical questions, reflect on the decisions they make, and be guided by us as they form their own professional identities. Seminars dedicated to creating space for professional reflection and formation serve a valuable role, but formation must be repeated and regularized throughout the curriculum.[67] What is needed is a methodology where this can take place in any subject-matter focused "doctrinal" course.

Fortunately, we already have that methodology—we just need to use it more. Teaching legal doctrine through simulations is a powerful and effective way of enabling professional formation because it is done in the context of the area of practice.[68] The *Carnegie Report* noted:

> While simulated practice can be an important site for developing skills and understandings essential for practice, it can also provide the setting for teaching the ethical demands of practice. Lawyering courses that use simulation of client interviewing and counseling, for example, permit the introduction of ethical as well as technical

64. *See* L. Sch. Survey of Student Engagement, LSSSE Law School Report 2014: Regent University School of Law 120 (2014) (identifying that 84.5 percent of Regent 3L's claim their law school experience "quite a bit" or "very much" helped them to develop a personal code of values and ethics, compared to only 54.3 percent of 3L's nationwide).

65. Colby & Sullivan, *supra* note 6, at 417.

66. *Id.*

67. *See* sources cited *supra* notes 44–47.

68. Carnegie Report, *supra* ch. 1, note 12, at 158–59.

> problems in a setting that mimics for the student the unpredictable challenges of actual practice.[69]

Indeed, teaching through simulations is becoming more common in other forms of professional education, particularly medical education: "It is instructive to note that . . . medical education has been moving heavily into the use of simulation."[70] Of course, medical education is different from legal education in many important ways, but the trend in medical education is "suggestive that increased use of the pedagogy of simulation is likely to prove a boon to teaching both practical skills and ethical-social development. Ethical engagement has practical dimensions that are more fully evident and can be examined and taught in conditions that simulate practice rather than in conventional classrooms."[71]

As has been noted, the *Carnegie Report* recommends that more courses be designed to provide the learning of doctrine *in the context of practice* and to present the legal principles in such a way that students are exposed to situations that allow them to begin to form their identities as legal professionals.[72] Simulated practice experiences delivered through doctrinal simulations are ideal for this.

The question then becomes what those "situations" might look like. This chapter offers a framework for contextual formation that should be applicable across the curriculum, from doctrinal classes to clinics. It involves a combination of guided steps that ideally take place in a particular order, called a Guidance Sequence for Formation of Professional Identity (GSFPI).

The sequence has four essential components: (1) a client representation, an exercise, or a writing assignment that presents an ethical dilemma as it appears in practice; (2) an identification by the student of the ethical quandary raised in completing the work; (3) a written expression by the student of the ethical issue as well as his reflection on his own decisions about how he resolved the dilemma; and (4) some form of written or oral feedback from the professor about the decisions and choices the student made and the quality and depth of the identification and reflection offered.

69. *Id.* at 158.

70. *Id.* at 159.

71. *Id.*

72. *Id.* at 195–97.

This could be accomplished fairly easily in any clinic, externship, or simulation-based course, but there is no reason it could not also be accomplished in a traditional doctrinal course as well. It could be a separate assignment in the course, with a portion of the grade assigned to it. The feedback from the professor is more time-consuming in a large class, but not impossible with a well-designed rubric. Offering such situations for students to engage with regularly throughout the course is ideal, and a whole-course simulation is the best form of this teaching. Still, if such methodologies were employed even once in every (or even most) doctrinal courses, it would go a long way to achieve the goals of the *Carnegie Report*'s intended integration.

We Need More Simulation Courses

It is possible to develop a model for upper class simulations that are designed to achieve the *Carnegie Report*'s call for integration of the three apprenticeships.[73] Such a model would be designed to integrate doctrine, skills, and professional identity formation in any law school course.[74] Typically taught in a simulation format, it can be applied to any legal doctrinal subject.[75] These courses can often provide necessary skills in a safe environment, and they can serve to prepare students to take a clinical course next, perhaps followed by an externship experience.

It is likely that these sorts of whole-course simulations—courses that intentionally integrate the three apprenticeships and use a systematic approach such as the GSFPI—may be the best pedagogy for the development of the third apprenticeship in our students, and the Carnegie Report expressly suggests

73. For an example of a whole-course simulation designed for this sort of integration, *see* Roberto L. Corrada, Teaching a Hybrid Administrative Law Simulation Using "Jurassic Park," (Forthcoming, J. Legal Educ. 2021). *See also* the Carnegie Report, *supra* ch. 1, note 12, at 12 (suggesting law schools adopt curricula that integrate the three apprenticeships throughout). The *Carnegie Report* also suggested that models for integration of the apprenticeships already existed in the legal writing programs of many law schools. Carnegie Report, *supra* ch. 1, note 12, at 104.

74. *Carnegie Integrated Courses*, *supra* note 73. For more information on the role of technology to support simulations, *see* Paul Maharg & Emma Nicol, Simulation and Technology in Legal Education: A Systematic Review and Future Research Programme in Caroline Strevens, Richard Grimes & Edward Phillips (eds.) Legal Education: Simulation in Theory and Practice (Ashgate 2014).

75. *Id.*

this is the case.[76] This is so because students learn the doctrine in the context that they apply it, so they are confronted with ethical issues as they arise in practice, and they must resolve them to complete the assignment and reflect on their formation.[77] While clinical and externship opportunities do this as well, it is challenging in those live-client representations to expose students to as many of the ethical issues that arise as can be done in the safer environment of a simulation.

Further, a simulation that places students in role relationships to each other—such as opposing counsel—creates a built-in benefit. Generally speaking, students are not willing to submit documents to each other that would be so sloppy or late as to inhibit the learning experience for their classmates. This might create a normative behavioral benefit: if their first experience (and then repeated experience) is in the mode and expectation of professional behavior, perhaps that will inculcate such behaviors as they enter practice.

With whole course simulations, we create a constructivist and learner-centered curriculum, which advances the twin goals of course integration and formation of professional identity. The resources are high in these courses—they require substantial individualized feedback—but with fewer resources directed toward the first year, faculty can be freed up to develop these sorts of courses, and they would find they enjoy teaching them more than the seventy-five person lecture class.

In the hybrid online model of legal education proposed in this book, there are even more opportunities for these sorts of simulations and creating a supportive learning environment for the formation of professional identity. If students are working on a "live" (but mock) case together (and perhaps as opposing counsel), it matters little that they be in the same room together all the time. Most practicing attorneys are not, after all. So gathering the entire class to orient them to the problem set(s), and then allowing them to work as lawyers with (and against) each other, creates a learning environment that facilitates the formation of professional identity in each student *and* models the hybrid work environment they are preparing to join.

---

76. Carnegie Report, supra ch. 1, note 12, at 26, 158–59.

77. The ABA counts simulations as experiential courses for the six required credits of experiential learning in Standard 303(a)(3), and in Standard 304(b) defines a simulation course as one "that is reasonably similar to the experience of a lawyer... representing a client."

Conclusion

By not intentionally creating opportunities for formation of our students' professional identities, we have sent an unmistakable message that this is not important, and that attorneys do not need to concern themselves with such worries, and arguably sending the message that they are preparing to be "hired hands." By not paying close attention to the identity dissonance that can affect students who may not fit the white, male paradigm of the profession, we are making law school even more difficult for many of those students. The *Carnegie Report* argues that the professionalism problem in the practice of law *starts in law school* and that it is not about mundane things like timeliness and respect for judges, but rather is founded in the professional identity of lawyers.[78] Further, it suggests that professional identity is governed only at its base by the Model Rules but is mostly about notions of duty and responsibility to society and the rule of law upon which that society is based.[79] The *Carnegie Report* called on law schools to give this third apprenticeship greater attention, focus, and intentionality, and to do so in a curriculum that integrates professional identity with the essential doctrinal knowledge and skills required to function as an attorney.[80] Whole-course simulations are ideal for achieving all of these goals.

When legal education is able to intentionally introduce opportunities for professional formation throughout law school—and honor the differing identities of their students rather than forcing a single paradigm of the successful attorney—and achieves apprenticeship integration in the second and third year, it will have moved substantially forward in addressing its obligation to prepare attorneys for a service profession in the twenty-first century, one that is committed to defending our democratic institutions and the rule of law. If legal education can change and adjust in these ways, it will have built a model for legal education that will be more successful for more students (and more diverse students) and this will—over time—increase the trust the public has in the profession.

---

78. *See* Carnegie Report, *supra* ch. 1, note 12, at 29–30.

79. *Id.* at 129.

80. *Id.* at 196.

FOUR

We Must Expand Experiential Learning in Law School

Introduction

Much of the focus of the changes that have been made in legal education over the last thirty years have been in the expansion of practical (sometimes called "practice-based") legal education. Many lawyers and some law professors have long believed that legal education placed too much emphasis on theoretical learning and not enough on practical learning.[1] The charge was made that we were graduating students who could *think* like a lawyer, but were unprepared to *be* a lawyer.[2] Law firms were expected to—and largely did—fill the gap, by offering essentially a training and transition year (or perhaps two), billing some of that time to their clients. But increasingly clients—particularly corporate clients—balked at paying for training and this became more difficult for law firms to take on, and thus they looked to law schools to do it for them.

---

1. Carnegie Report *supra* ch.1, note 12, at 8 ("[O]ne of the less happy legacies of the inherited academic ideology has been a history of unfortunate misunderstandings and even conflict between defenders of theoretical legal learning and champions of a legal education that includes introduction to the practice of law."). Portions of this chapter were originally published in David I. C. Thomson, *Defining Experiential Learning*, 1 J. Exp. Learning 1 (2014–15), and is reprinted here with permission.

2. David Segal, *What They Don't Teach Law Students: Lawyering*, N.Y. Times (Nov. 20, 2011) at A1.

Of course, practical training was the only kind available until about 1870, so practical legal education is not new.[3] Law schools for decades have included in their standard curricula opportunities for students to apply their theoretical learning to real clients. Over the last several decades, the widely accepted clinical pedagogy has matured and strengthened,[4] and the status of those who teach this part of the curriculum has improved.[5] Clinical education is a valuable and important part of legal education, and always will be. If the problem with legal education is that students have little or no experience of practice before they graduate, then giving them some of that in a clinic is an obvious improvement. Representing a real client while in school is an invaluable learning experience, and important to the professional formation of our students—just as is the study of tort law and learning how to read and interpret cases is important. Legal education has long had strength in doctrinal teaching and—for those students who could avail themselves of a clinical experience—some practical teaching as well. The two aspects of the curriculum often did not interact or integrate, but at least there was strength in both areas.

Alas, we have come to understand that legal practice—and thus good legal training—does not operate as a duality but rather involves a rich tapestry with layers of complexity in virtually every day. And thus, the best legal education should not operate as a duality either. Purely doctrinal lecture courses (how

3. *See generally*, *e.g.*, Robert Stevens, Law School: Legal Education in America from the 1850s to 1980s (Univ. N. Carolina Press 1983).

4. *See, e.g.*, Anne-Marie Cavazos, *The Journey Toward Excellence in Clinical Legal Education: Developing, Utilizing and Evaluating Methodologies for Determining and Assessing the Effectiveness of Student Learning Outcomes*, 40 Sw. U. L. Rev. 1 (2010); Phyllis Goldfarb, *Back to the Future of Clinical Legal Education*, 32 B.C. J.L. & Soc. Just. 279 (2012); Carolyn Grose, *Beyond Skills Training, Revisited: The Clinical Education Spiral*, 19 Clinical L. Rev. 489 (2013) (contains extensive footnotes citing classics of clinical pedagogy). *See also*, J.P. Ogilvy, *Clinical Legal Education: An Annotated Bibliography*, 11 Clinical L. Rev. (Special Issue No. 2) 10, 10–20 (2005) (annotated bibliography of articles about clinical pedagogy and methodology).

5. *See* Bryan L. Adamson et al., *Clinical Faculty in the Legal Academy: Hiring, Promotion and Retention*, 62 J. Legal Educ. 115, 131 (2012) (report of AALS Task Force on the Status of Clinicians and the Legal Academy finding, as one of several core principles, that "[t]he legal academy and profession benefit from full inclusion of clinical faculty on all matters affecting the mission, function, and direction of law schools. . . ."); Todd Berger, *Three Generations and Two Tiers: How Participation in Law School Clinics and the Demand for "Practice-Ready" Graduates Will Impact the Faculty Status of Clinical Law Professors*, 43 Wash. U. J.L. & Pol'y 129, 132 (2014) (arguing that "the growing importance of clinical education increases the likelihood clinical law professors will achieve equality with non-clinical faculty.").

property law is often taught, for example) with the addition of a purely clinical experience do not (alone) make for an integrated learning environment that mimics the diversity of skills and experience needed for competent legal practice. As the calls for greater exposure to practical experience in law school have increased, those schools that have merely added an additional clinic or two and thought their work was done are learning that their approach was incomplete.[6]

Most law schools have known this and have already made some adjustments. Every law school has trial practice classes, for example. These courses do not involve a live client matter, but they simulate the trial experience well and most students who have taken such a course and happen to appear in court soon after graduation feel at least somewhat prepared to do so. Further, an enterprising professor of employment law[7] has applied the simulation model to teach employment law transactions in a similar way, so that graduates who might join a corporate firm will be familiar with—and even somewhat skilled at—identifying the key aspects of an employment contract or an employee handbook and assisting with the negotiation and drafting of a new one. What is needed is an even greater variety of experiential opportunities that speaks to the strengths of our faculty and the needs of our students, and that is nuanced in its delivery by subject matter or specialty area of law.

It turns out that prospective law students know this, and increasingly are looking for schools that will provide a robust opportunity to learn through experience. A three-year study of the Experiential Advantage Program at Denver's Sturm College of Law revealed strong preference for learning through experiential courses, and that many students had selected the school, in part, on that basis.[8] And as they were leaving, these students perceived value in those courses, and that their law school helped them to get a job and be prepared for doing that job well.[9]

---

6. It may also be impractical for reasons of cost. *See* Martin J. Katz, *Understanding the Costs of Experiential Legal Education*, 1 J. Experiential Learning 28, 30 (2014).

7. Rachel S. Arnow-Richman, *Employment as Transaction*, 39 Seton Hall L. Rev. 447, 447 (2009).

8. David I. C. Thomson & Stephen Daniels, *If You Build It They Will Come: What Students Say About Experiential Learning*, 13 Fla. A&M U. L. Rev. 203, 219–23 (2018).

9. *Id.* at 238–39.

A Brief History of Experiential Learning

Experience-based learning of this sort is not new—it finds its roots in the work of the early twentieth century philosopher and educator John Dewey, who addressed himself in some of his work to extolling the benefits of experience-based learning. Dewey believed that the central dilemma of education is to acquaint the young "with the past in such a way that the acquaintance is a potent agent in appreciation of a living present,"[10] and that one of the best ways to do this was to expose students to the experience of the working world of which they were soon going to be a part. Dewey noted that "the central problem of an education based upon experience is to select the kind of present experiences that live fruitfully and creatively in subsequent experiences."[11]

"Experiential learning," as it came to be known, became quite popular in secondary education in the middle of the twentieth century, and its influence is still quite profound there over fifty years later. Throughout public and private secondary schools, teachers introduce contextual learning exercises, field trips, and immersive lab experiences in nearly every subject. But it is only fairly recently that these principles have been applied to a developing spectrum of courses that law schools are now making available to their students.

This discussion has become all the more important because the American Bar Association, which accredits law schools, now requires all law students to take six credits of experiential courses as part of their course of study.[12] As with many such periods of significant growth and change, however, some classification and a deeper understanding of the types and methods of experiential learning in law schools would be helpful. This chapter offers a definition of experiential learning for legal education, as well as a method for application of the definition to courses currently in the law school curriculum and considered for inclusion in the curriculum of the future.

---

10. John Dewey, Experience and Education 23 (Free Press 1938).

11. *Id.* at 27–28.

12. A.B.A. Section of Legal Educ. & Admissions to the Bar, Revised Standards for Approval of Law Schools, Standard 303(a)(3) (2022) available at http://www.americanbar.org/content/dam/aba/administrative/legal_education_and_admissions_to_the_bar/council_reports_and_resolutions/201406_revised_standards_clean_copy.authcheckdam.pdf.

It Is Not Just the Clinic

For many of those years, experiential education in law was thought to be limited to the clinical experience. Embedded in this view was the assumption that experiential education was about exposing students to the experience of representing a "live" client. The term "live client" refers to a client with a real, active legal problem that the student will work—as that client's attorney—to help resolve. But while this form of experiential education is a valuable one it is not the only one. In the last twenty years or so, other forms of experiential education have grown up around clinical education, aimed at grounding a student's legal education in experience, although not necessarily with a live client.

And so, as recently as five or ten years ago, a typical "traditional" faculty member at most law schools would likely—if asked—put experiential education into two (perhaps three) neat boxes: clinics, externships, and (perhaps) simulations. The same faculty member might also be able to describe each in their most common form. A classic example of a clinic might be an immigration clinic that assigns students to represent clients in immigration hearings, with a clinical faculty member overseeing their work. The faculty member might also be able to describe a classic example of an externship as a judicial externship, arranged by an externship coordinator (typically a member of the staff), where a student spends part of the week in the chambers of a judge, helping with legal research, and occasionally helping during court hearings. Finally, the classic example of a simulation would be Trial Practice, often taught by prominent trial attorneys in the community, almost entirely in the form of a simulated trial, with little lecture and much more "stand up" experience for each student with portions of a typical trial: opening statements, direct and cross examinations, and closing statements. While examples of these sorts still exist in most law schools, part of the current renaissance in experiential education can be found in the hybridization, extension, and broadening of these learning opportunities. The increased variety of experiential learning in legal education is generally a good thing, but it makes this effort to define it more complex.

The first year legal writing class entered the curriculum approximately thirty years ago. Since then, the pedagogy of the course has grown and matured, and a great deal of significant scholarship has been published about how to teach it well, develop its learning outcomes, and conduct effective assessment.[13]

13. *E.g.*, Daniel L. Barnett, *Triage in the Trenches of the Legal Writing Course: The Theory and Methodology of Analytical Critique*, 38 U. Tol. L. Rev. 651 (2007); Paul Brest, *A*

While the course is in some schools still titled "Legal Research and Writing," most faculty members who teach in this area consider this to no longer be a representative term for what is now addressed by this course (although it does include both of those subjects). Some schools have changed the name of the course to Lawyering Process. This title is intentionally descriptive of what the course addresses and how it does so. It is taught almost entirely with simulated client problems and is designed to introduce first year students broadly to the *process* that *lawyers* go through to do their jobs. This process includes client interviewing, statute and case reading, legal analysis, legal research, and several forms of legal expression, including legal writing, contract drafting, and oral advocacy. The course is designed to provide the critical foundational lawyering skills for each student, whatever area of practice they might enter. All lawyers must know how to write and speak about the law they have found relevant to a client matter to different audiences, and this is the foundation upon which most of the rest of law school, and every legal career, rests. It is also where the groundwork for the formation of professional identity of each student is laid.

As noted in Chapter Three, formation of a student's professional identity is not something that can be taught, didactically. In the lawyering course professors must create engaging learning opportunities in which their students are forced to make those choices—above the line—about where they want to live their future lives as lawyers. Practical legal education of all kinds (including clinics, externships, etc.) is all about putting the student in the role of the lawyer and setting high expectations for behavior and product. It is impractical to expect to achieve such goals in first-year doctrinal classes, and so this is yet another reason why the lawyering course is so important. This book proposes that the lawyering course as we currently think of it move to the second year

---

First-Year Course in the "Lawyering Process," 32 J. Leg. Educ. 344 (1982); Kristen K. Davis, *Designing and Using Peer Review in a First-Year Legal Research and Writing Course*, 9 J. Legal Writing 1 (2003); Susan J. Hankin, *Bridging Gaps and Blurring Lines: Integrating Analysis, Writing, Doctrine, and Theory*, 17 Legal Writing: J. Legal Writing Inst. 325 (2011); Soma R. Kedia, *Redirecting the Scope of First-Year Writing Courses: Toward a New Paradigm of Teaching Legal Writing*, 87 U. Det. Mercy L. Rev. 147 (2010); Ellie Margolis and Susan L. DeJarnatt, *Moving Beyond Product to Process: Building a Better LRW Program*, 46 Santa Clara L. Rev. 93 (2005); David S. Romantz, *The Truth About Cats and Dogs: Legal Writing Courses and the Law School Curriculum*, 52 U. Kan. L. Rev. 105 (2003); Lucia Ann Silecchia, *Legal Skills Training in the First Year of Law School: Research? Writing? Analysis? Or More?*, 100 Dick. L. Rev. 245 (1996).

of law school, with an introduction to legal writing and professional formation in the first year of hybrid online instruction.

In the lawyering course, each student must start the process of transitioning from being a student working toward a grade to a lawyer trying to solve a problem for a client. Much of that transition begins in that course. It happens through the work assigned, and the client problems students are working to solve, and through role-playing by the students in client interviewing, counseling, and presenting an oral argument. Because the lawyering course is taught almost entirely in simulation format, the lawyering faculty at each school has valuable experience in teaching with simulations, a fact that has been overlooked at some schools in the past. As more schools seek to add more simulation courses to their curricula, they should look to their lawyering faculty for help and expertise.[14]

In the second year of law school, a robust lawyering course would be combined with clinical pedagogy, which is also well established. Most clinics are focused in areas of law—civil or criminal litigation, civil rights litigation, or representation of community organizations. These clinics involve "live" clients with active legal matters. They include a classroom component and close supervision by a clinical faculty member. Increasingly, however, there are cooperative hybrid clinics emerging in law schools. An example would be a non-clinical doctrinal faculty member entering into a representation agreement with a client for some limited appellate work on a novel case and managing students through some representational aspects of that work. Another example could be the lawyering course representing a "live" client non-profit organization, by conducting legal research and writing that might be helpful to the organization in ongoing litigation in which it is involved.[15]

Externships, where students work for a judge, assistant district attorney, or in a law office, used to be mostly a placement function. Today, accepted externship pedagogy involves faculty instruction in a classroom component to every externship opportunity, and some training for the practitioner supervising attorneys. Further, while externships used to include the equivalent of three to five credit hours of work outside the law school, an emerging form of externship involves the student spending the entire semester, and earning

14. For a detailed look at how the Lawyering Process course is designed and taught, including opportunities for the formation of professional identity, *see* David I. C. Thomson, *What We Do: The Life and Work of The Legal Writing Professor*, 50:2 J.L. & Educ. 703 (2021).

15. Nantiya Ruan, *Experiential Learning in the First Year Curriculum: The Public Interest Partnership*, 8 JALWD 191, 203 (2011).

fifteen credits, working onsite on an externship assignment.[16] While this seems new, in fact, it is not—Northeastern Law School pioneered the "cooperative" model of legal education many years ago, whereby students alternate semesters between being in school and working in the "field." While this approach initially seemed to be an outlier approach to legal education, more schools are experimenting with the "semester-in-practice" model.

One of the many advantages to moving the law school curriculum to a more hybrid online format is that it opens up numerous opportunities for experiential pedagogy. One might think the opposite: that experiential learning has to take place within a mock courtroom, or a clinic office, for example. But a hybrid learning environment allows for greater flexibility in creating learning moments, particularly of the kind that experiential learning prefers. That is, if the goal is for the student to experience being in role as an attorney, this can be done in myriad ways. For example, a deposition or court hearing can be conducted online. A video feed of a trial being conducted in a place not convenient for the student to travel can serve as the experience of attending a trial. The great advantage of such hybrid modes of instruction today is that so much of legal practice is conducted this way. It already was before Covid, but it is even more common post-Covid. Thus, students get the same learning experience, but also *in one of the ways* they will be practicing law in their future.

The hybridization, extension, and broadening of experiential legal education makes any attempt to define "experiential learning" in the context of law schools complex and problematic. But define it we must, as it is a critical component of the way forward for the second and third years of legal education as envisioned in this book.

A Proposed Definition of Experiential Learning

For the reasons noted above, a new definition of experiential learning is needed, one that is focused on the student experience, is inclusive of future developments, and is broad enough to encompass the many forms of experi-

16. For example, the University of Denver offers a Semester in Practice, which is a full-immersion, 15-credit externship. *See* Semester in Practice, Univ. Denver, Sturm Coll. L., Legal Externship Program https://www.law.du.edu/sites/default/files/2019-07/Sip-handout-for-supervisors-2019.pdf (last visited, August 14, 2022).

ential learning that are already available in law schools across the country.[17] Accordingly, this book offers the following definition of experiential learning opportunities in the context of legal education:

> The term "Experiential Learning" refers to methods of instruction that regularly or primarily place students in the role of attorneys, whether through simulations, clinics, or externships. Such forms of instruction integrate theory and practice by providing numerous opportunities for students to learn and apply lawyering skills as they are used in legal practice (or similar professional settings). These learning opportunities are also designed to encourage students to begin to form their professional identities as lawyers, through experience or role-playing with guided self-reflection, so that they can become skilled, ethical, and professional life-long learners of the law.

This definition has several essential attributes. The first and foremost is that it focuses on the student experience not the faculty function. Second, it has at its core the placement of students *in the role of attorneys*. So any course that places students in role of attorneys doing what lawyers do can be an experiential course. Third, it emphasizes the importance of the Carnegie third apprenticeship, the *formation of professional identity*, in the hope that this will become a more intentional aspect of this pedagogy. Finally, it underscores that what we are doing in law school is not merely imparting a closed set of legal principles to our students, but rather foundational concepts upon which they can build their legal careers in the ever-changing legal landscape of their future and that a critical part of doing so is becoming life-long learners of the law.[18]

---

17. Portions of this Chapter were previously published in David I. C. Thomson, *Defining Experiential Learning*, 1 J. Experiential Learning 1 (2014–15), and are reprinted here with permission.

18. The concept of lifelong learning skills being a goal of the educational enterprise also finds its roots in the work of John Dewey, who believed that "Collateral learning in the way of formation of enduring attitudes...may be and often is much more important that the spelling lesson or lesson in geography or history that is learned. For these attitudes are fundamentally what count in the future. The most important attitude that can be formed is that of desire to go on learning." Dewey, *supra* note 10, at 48. Portions of this definition and its application were developed by the author in collaboration with the Experiential Learning Committee at Denver Law in 2010.

Applying the Definition

When applying this definition to an existing curriculum, schools might find that faculty members want to use this definition to suggest that their primarily traditional theory course is now an experiential learning course. Faculty members might argue that by means of the traditional "Socratic" method of teaching, they are placing their students "in role" as attorneys by asking many of the questions they typically ask during the regular class time. Including such a course is not the intention of this definition, but because it is not designed to exclude certain types of law teaching, that might not be clear. Further, the definition contains a bias that faculty members should be able to make their own determinations in good faith that their courses are experiential in nature,[19] and will need to be able to do so should they want to gradually transition from a traditional mode of teaching to a more experiential one. So further guidance is necessary to separate those courses that truly belong on the experiential side of the spectrum—and those courses that belong on the other side—while this transition is taking place in many of the courses in a typical law school's curriculum.

Accordingly, this definition includes a set of questions that are designed to sharpen the definition in application to particular courses in the curriculum. Those questions, with brief explanations of each, are:

> Other than the question-based format in a mostly lecture-based class, do you place students in the role of attorneys through problems or exercises where they act as attorneys—such as drafting documents or interacting with (for example) either assigned co-counsel or opposing counsel?

---

19. This suggestion is made for internal transitional purposes, not for ABA regulatory purposes. Under this proposal, each law school's Associate Dean of Academic Affairs, or Associate Dean of Experiential Learning, would still have to respond to the ABA's annual request for information and make a reasonable determination based on the ABA's definitions. During a transitional period, however, this chapter suggests that for internal curricular purposes at most law schools, faculty should be able to designate their courses as fitting the definition provided here, and it assumes that they would do this in good faith. Without such an approach, an Associate Dean or Curriculum Committee risks serving as an arbiter of a definitional line that could come too close to threatening traditional notions of academic freedom.

The idea behind this question is probably obvious; it intentionally excludes mostly lecture-based classes. However, if a faculty member includes "in role" exercises such as the given examples, the course could be considered experiential, depending on how often such exercises are included, which leads to the next question.

If so, does your class design use this teaching technique regularly or primarily throughout the course?

The terminology "regularly or primarily" may seem imprecise, of course, but it is intended to convey the idea that an experiential course does not include such exercises rarely or occasionally, and it connects to the Best Practices report's use of the terms "significant or primary."[20] But here, "regularly" connotes something that happens in a pattern more than once, and in the Best Practices definition "significant" is less instructive, since what is deemed significant by one faculty member might be considered insignificant by another. The thinking behind using "regularly" is that a course where such instruction is regular (as opposed to occasional) is one that is more likely to be experiential in nature. It remains, however, imprecise, but this is by design. This definition (and the questions that follow it) seeks to put considerable discretion in the hands of faculty members, where academic freedom dictates it should reside, while still providing as much guidance as possible.

Do you include opportunities for student self-reflection (in writing) about the experience of being "in role" so as to help them form their professional identities as lawyers?

This question tests whether there are intentionally designed opportunities for student reflection on the formation of professional identity during the course. This is not a requirement of the definition, but if the answer to this question is affirmative, the course would obviously be more aligned with the definition than if it is not. However, it is possible for a course—such as Trial Practice—where there was no such opportunity for reflection to still be an

20. Stuckey, *supra* ch. 1, note 57, at 121. Note that the ABA Requirement for each student to complete 6 credits of experiential learning applies to instruction that is "primarily experiential in nature," and includes courses that "integrate doctrine, theory, skills and legal ethics." A.B.A. Standards and Rules of Procedure for Approval of Law Schools, Standard 304 (a)(1).

experiential course. But such opportunities abound in a Trial Practice course, and merely adding some intentional structure around those opportunities for formation of professional identity as a trial lawyer would quickly answer this question in the affirmative.

Also, by asking this question, law professors can determine whether they have adequately planned for the formation of professional identity in their students through opportunities of student reflection. Although self-reflection is not *required* by the definition, a course that plans these opportunities meets at least one of the goals of experiential education. Obviously, courses absent opportunities for students to reflect, but with other structures in place for students to form their professional identities, can still be classified as "experiential."[21] This could also be true of virtually any course in the law school curriculum. Any course could incorporate one or more designed modules[22] that fit the substantive area of law being taught.

Is a substantial portion of the student's grade in the course based on your evaluation of these exercises or learning opportunities?

Finally, this question gets to the heart of the matter, although it still does so with some room for discretion on the part of the faculty member. Without a substantial portion of the grade being at stake in experience-based exercises and reflection, the exercises would seem (to this definition) be more of an attempt to "bolt-on" experiential learning, rather than it being an integrated part of the course design. A common phrase among assessment professionals is that "we should measure what we value."[23] It is the intention of this definition that experiential exercises be integrated into the course and carry grade weight

---

21. Any practice-heavy courses such as trial or pre-trial practice would require only a bit of planning to convert them into explicitly identity formation courses.

22. *See supra* ch. 3 for a discussion of this teaching methodology.

23. Robert Coe & Carol Taylor Fitz-Gibbon, *School Effectiveness Research: Criticisms and Recommendations*, 24 Oxford Rev. of Educ. 421, 433 (2006). For discussions of assessing learning outcomes and student performance, *see generally* Carnegie Report *supra* ch.1, note 12; Andrea A. Curcio, *Assessing Differently and Using Empirical Studies to See If It Makes a Difference: Can Law Schools Do It Better?*, 27 Quinnipiac L. Rev. 899 (2009); Janet W. Fisher, *Putting Students at the Center of Legal Education: How an Emphasis on Outcome Measures in the ABA Standards for Approval of Law Schools Might Transform the Educational Experience of Law Students*, 35 S. Ill. U. L.J. 225 (2011); Rogelio Lasso, *Is Our Students Learning? Using Assessments to Measure and Improve Law School Learning and Performance*, 15 Barry L. Rev. 73 (2010); Herbert N. Ramy, *Moving Students from Hearing and Forgetting to Doing and Understanding: A Manual for Assessment in Law School*, 41 Cap. U. L. Rev. 837 (2013).

so that students will know that the teacher values these exercises, and that they are an integral part of achieving the learning objectives for the course.

This definition of experiential learning, which includes and should be taken together with the follow-on questions, is intended to help associate deans, curriculum committees, and law faculty members to determine what courses they currently have in the curriculum that qualify as experiential learning opportunities for their students. In applying the definition, they may find that they have more such courses than they thought, and faculty members might be encouraged by this definition to add experiential components to their classes.

Having offered this definition of experiential learning, being more specific about the various *types* or sub-categories of experiential learning opportunities is more problematic. This is because, as noted, the types of experiential learning are growing and changing and a significant amount of hybridization is underway. In spite of that, the three archetypes of experiential education in law—simulations, externships, and clinics—remain useful for general categorization purposes. Further, attempts to precisely define each sub-category of experiential learning in law schools seems artificial and limiting and driven more by faculty interests than student needs.

Instead, perhaps the better way to classify types of experiential learning is to focus on the student experience by looking first at the nature of the client contact, second at the form of representation, and finally at the type of supervision being provided.

First, is there client contact? If there is none, it is probably not an experiential course. If the course is designed to expose students to simulated client contact, then it is a simulation. Finally, if there is live client contact (directly or indirectly), then it is probably a clinic or an externship.

Second, what is the nature of the representation being provided by the student? Is there representation of an actual client? If a simulated client is being represented, then it is a simulation. If it is a live client, is the representation being conducted under a local student practice act? If so, it is probably a clinical experience. If there is a "live" client but the representation is being offered at some remove—such as drafting portions of appellate briefs in the context of a doctrinal class—then it is a hybrid clinical course. If there is a less direct form of representation, then it is probably an externship.

Third, what is the type of supervision the student is receiving? If a full-time faculty member is providing the supervision, then it is either a simulation or a clinic (or it is in course work for an externship). If it is an adjunct, it is likely a simulation. If it is a non-faculty member, it is probably an externship.

Conclusion

Over the last 20 years, experiential learning has expanded throughout legal education, and for good reason. Merely studying each legal subject is not enough. Some experience applying the legal principles being studied not only supports the learning of the subject at hand, but also prepares the student to take on real clients and client matters after graduation. Accordingly, this book proposes that the second and third years of law school be spent primarily in experiential learning courses, such as simulation courses (where the students in placed in the role of an attorney, but with a mock client), clinical courses (with an actual client matter), and externships—even to the extent of the full semester in practice under the supervision of a practicing attorney, preferably in an area of practice of interest to the student.

While it might seem at first an obstacle, continuing the transition to hybrid online learning environments actually helps us to do this. Because a hybrid learning environment that has been developed to be optimized for that form of delivery can creatively bring in experiential learning opportunities in online formats. The great advantage of doing this is that it will prepare students for the practice lives they will be leading, because in so many ways, their future practice lives will be hybrid, with some in-person elements and some online.

FIVE

The Future Is Hybrid

Introduction

The title of this chapter should strike the reader as a little odd. Or perhaps merely obvious. Because today our lives are already hybrid—a mix of in-person and online—in so many ways. So, the present is hybrid. But examining what this means, and specifically what it means for the way forward for legal education, is what this chapter addresses. This book argues that the path forward in legal education will be hybrid, and should be, for many reasons. We are not going back to in-person classes and in-person office hours for every student interaction ever again. It was already moving in that direction before the Covid pandemic, but the pandemic accelerated it. And now, the primarily in-person form of teaching graduate school (at least) is in the past. It is instructive to first examine how ubiquitous hybridization has become in our lives, and then turn to how this will play out in legal education.

If we casually look around, we see that we are already living a hybrid life. Many of us still drive an analog car, but we use a navigation system to find our way. We still write handwritten grocery lists, but we keep our calendar on our phones. We can receive a call or a photo on our watches (*Dick Tracy* style[1]), and we love the convenience of the Kindle, but we still read paper books.

We can lament these changes. We can worry about how far it goes. But our lives today are a rich and variable mixture of in-person and digital interactions,

1. *See* Michael Daly, *How Dick Tracy Invented the Apple Watch*, Daily Beast (Apr. 14, 2017, 11:53AM ET), https://www.thedailybeast.com/how-dick-tracy-invented-the-apple-watch.

and this is not likely to change. The question is whether it is good for our society, and good for education. This chapter argues it is, on balance, good for both.

The Hybrid Work World

Today, most knowledge workers—including law professors and administrators—live the hybrid life. We work from home a couple of days per week, we attend our child's soccer game in-person (now that we have more flexibility to allow for that), and we have family dinner, but then we join a group at our church or chair a committee meeting at the local food bank—with some members attending in person, and some on Zoom. But on Saturday, we play a softball game with friends, and that night, attend a live concert, but remotely—at home.

For at least the last decade—probably two—many knowledge-workers have worked a day here and there remotely from home. Computer power and internet bandwidth to the home has been more than sufficient to manage this since at least 2005. Video conferencing software has been reasonably reliable for nearly a decade, and the computing power and bandwidth to support it has also been widely available for a long time. We bought computers for the home—for games, budgets, Amazon orders—and soon we were able to check work email from home.

When the video-conferencing software Skype came out in 2003 it was used sporadically.[2] Not everyone had a camera and microphone that would make it useable. As we do with new technologies, we gradually got used to it, and accepted the concept of video conferencing until it was not new anymore. When nearly all laptops and desktops included cameras and microphones—around 2010—videoconferencing finally became more mainstream. Zoom debuted in 2012 and became known as "Skype that works."[3] And when the Covid pandemic caused us to move so much online, so quickly, it seemed like the world moved to Zoom all at once. And now we can no longer imagine *not* having built-in cameras, microphones, and Zoom—and powerful computers to run them—in our homes.

---

2. *Skype*, britannica.com, https://www.britannica.com/technology/Skype (last visited Aug. 31, 2022).

3. Walter S. Mossberg, *A Chance to Call 15 Friends to Video Chat in High Def*, Wall Street J. (Aug. 21, 2012, 9:01 PM ET), https://www.wsj.com/articles/SB10000872396390444435045776033832386l6426.

We prepare our students to be lawyers, and for the most part, we still think they will be working in a traditional office of some sort. For at least 100 years, the workplace has held a mythic and powerful hold on our lives. Going to an office every day was just what we did, what was expected, what we needed to do to get work done. It was often where we met our friend group, and social events took place like potlucks and birthday cakes and retirement parties. We had managers and bosses who wanted to see us, and have meetings, and we needed to consult our fellow workers and learn from them and they from us.

We can now see that the shift to remote work during the pandemic was a profound and important change—to those of us in legal education and to our students. The technology—and our familiarity with it—had matured well before 2020, so it was ready for us to switch over to it out of necessity. Managers and bosses were nervous—this was out of their comfort zone, because they could not see their employees anymore, or not in the same way or at the same frequency. But their hand was forced—they did not have any other options.[4] Before the pandemic, managers and workers could not really conceive of a world in which workers did not have to come into the office regularly.

And then millions of employees shifted to working from home, and something incredibly powerful happened. The business world and most law firms (and government offices) continued, and in many cases, continued to prosper. And workers were happier because we were not wasting time in difficult commutes, and they had more time with their children and other pursuits.[5]

Managers and bosses find themselves in a very difficult spot. They are not entirely comfortable with either remote work or the shift in leverage it has given their workers.[6] The ephemera of what they do—oversee and manage—is indelibly place-based in their minds. But the evidence is in front of us: remote work works.[7] Of course, there may be training needs, and occasional in-person events. But workers can be, and have been, productive at home for

---

4. *See* Sharon K. Parker et al., *Remote Managers Are Having Trust Issues*, Harv. Bus. Rev. (2020), https://netfamilybusiness.com/wp-content/uploads/2020/08/Remote-Managers-Are-Having-Trust-Issues.pdf.

5. *See* Adi Gaskell, *Research Explores the Economic Benefits of Remote Work During Covid-19*, Forbes (Feb 15, 2022, 8:45 AM EST), https://www.forbes.com/sites/adigaskell/2022/02/15/research-explores-the-economic-benefits-of-remote-work-during-covid/?sh=73441be776cc.

6. *See* Parker, *supra* note 4.

7. *See* Sean Peek, *Communication Technology and Inclusion Will Shape the Future of Remote Work*, Bus. News Daily (Aug. 12, 2022), https://www.businessnewsdaily.com/8156-future-of-remote-work.html.

many years.[8] And many, many, businesses have not just survived but prospered. As much as some might like to say we have to go back to "normal," it seems very unlikely to happen. With a few minor exceptions, there is little evidence that it should.

To be fair, quite a few companies have seen this reality with great clarity and made bold moves. Price Waterhouse Coopers, a big four accounting firm with 285,000 employees, has announced that it will be converting everyone to remote work.[9] Allstate Insurance, a company with $45 billion in revenue, has closed most of its regional offices around the US, and has put its headquarters campus north of Chicago up for sale.[10] Both companies will still have offices for some purposes, but just those two recent data points should bring the point home. The landscape of work has dramatically changed. This has profound implications for those of us who work in law schools.[11]

First, if remote work and videoconferencing technologies have become mainstream—and they have—the historical objections to online and hybrid education fall apart. Second, a big chunk of what our education system has done for a hundred years (at least) is prepare workers to be productive in the workplace. If the workplace changes in such a profound way, we will have changes to make to prepare our students for this new landscape.

One of the most important things we have discovered in remote and hybrid work is how it has affected BIPOC knowledge workers. A recent survey of 10,000 workers found that 97 percent of black knowledge workers do not want to be in the office full time, as opposed to 79 percent of white workers.[12] Further, positive responses to questions during the remote work period of the pan-

8. *See* Mohamad Adawa et al., *Working from Home During the COVID-19 Pandemic: Impact on Office Worker Productivity and Work Experience*, IOS Press 1171, 1182–83 (2021) available at https://content.iospress.com/download/work/wor210301?id=work%2Fwor210301.

9. Jessica DiNapoli, *Exclusive PwC Offers U.S. Employees Full-time Remote Work*, Reuters (Sept. 30, 2021), https://www.reuters.com/business/exclusive-pwc-tells-us-employees-they-need-never-return-office-2021-09-30/.

10. David Roeder, *Allstate to Sell Northbrook Site to Warehouse Builder*, Chi. Sun Times (Nov. 29, 2021), https://chicago.suntimes.com/business/2021/11/29/22807757/allstate-headquarters-campus-northbrook-sale-warehouse-developer-dermody-properties.

11. *See, e.g.*, Timothy Casey, *Reflections on Legal Education in the Aftermath of a Pandemic*, 28 Clinical L. Rev. 85, 89–90 (2021).

12. Sheela Subramanian, *A New Era of Workplace Inclusion: Moving from Retrofit to Redesign*, Future Forum, Slack (Mar. 11, 2021), https://futureforum.com/2021/03/11/dismantling-the-office-moving-from-retrofit-to-redesign/.

demic that were designed to measure "sense of belonging" *increased* for people of color.[13] The uncomfortable reality is that such workers are often subjected to various micro-aggressions in the workplace, passed over for promotions, and their contributions are often overlooked and/or undermined.[14] It is racial bias, full stop. And it is pervasive in the workplace.[15] But what we have (preliminarily) learned is that BIPOC workers have found that they prefer remote work, perhaps because it reduces the opportunities for micro-aggressions that used to take place in the office.[16] This perhaps may be, in part, because when the team meets on Zoom, everyone's box is the same size, and the uses of the chat box can also be a leveler.

We Need More Hybrid Teaching

For us in legal education, pre-pandemic, the debate was about online versus in-person instruction. But it not an either/or choice. The goal is *hybrid* instruction, just like everything else in our lives, and the new work world our students will join. During the period of "emergency remote teaching" many of us missed the opportunity to learn how to use online instruction more effectively and to make our teaching more student centered and personalized. We were just too rushed, and dragged our in-person teaching methods into the digital realm, whether that fit well or not. But accepting that the future of legal instruction is hybrid is our best way forward. There is an incredibly interesting discussion we need to be having in education about how to mix what technology is good at with what in-person is good at. But the switch back and forth between one or the other—in a binary fashion—has been sub-optimal for everyone, students and teachers alike. And because of that, we have fallen into a state of surviving but not thriving.

If we are honest with ourselves, the legal educational system we designed over the last century involved a lot of generic herding and sorting of large groups of students. We knew it was not ideal, because we have always known that students are not cattle, but rather individuals with different backgrounds,

13. *Id.*

14. Laura Morgan Roberts & Anthony J. Mayo, *Towards a Racially Just Workplace*, Harv. Bus. Rev. (November 14, 2019), https://hbr.org/2019/11/toward-a-racially-just-workplace.

15. *Id.*

16. *See* Subramanian, *supra* note 12.

needs, and motivations.[17] One of the great things about the recent shift to online—as abrupt and painful as it has been—is that we have become more nuanced and compassionate as teachers with our students. We were experiencing a painful time ourselves, and so we understood that our students are as well. Instead of reflexively thinking, "What is wrong with you?", we are instead thinking, "What has happened—what is going on with you?" It is a world of difference, and we need more of it.

Unfortunately, much of our hybrid instruction so far has been "stuck at substitution." That is, we are trying to recreate the in-class experience in the cloud, without taking the time to think through what parts of the in-class experience could be improved by the smart use of online technologies. A helpful frame with which to think of this problem is the **SAMR** model.[18] The goal we want to get to is illustrated as follows: we want to move from **S**ubstitution, to **A**ugmentation, to **M**odification, and finally to **R**edefinition.

Augmentation is the next step from mere substitution, where we might take a problem description and make it the subject of a breakout group, then put it on Google Docs for a collaborative exercise to solve or improve it.[19] **M**odification involves redesigning the student task you used to assign in a way that gives students more freedom to show mastery outside of the "paper and pencil,"[20] perhaps through a video they develop or a podcast interview. It is when we truly reimagine how to achieve each learning goal that we reach **R**edefinition—a completely different way of interacting with the instructional material than what we used before, one that emphasizes quality engagement over seat time, and offers the student greater autonomy support.[21]

If these ideas and concepts are new to you as a law professor or administrator, they are not new to the instructional designer you probably have available to help you. Most universities today have instructional designers who specialize in adding hybrid components to previously "traditional"

---

17. *See* Casey, *supra* note 11 at 96–97.

18. The SAMR model was developed by Dr. Reuben Puentedura. For more information, *see* Rueben Puentedura, *Technology is Learning*, https://sites.google.com/a/msad60.org/technology-is-learning/samr-model (last visited Sept. 1, 2022).

19. *Id.*

20. *Id.*

21. *See generally*, Kennon M. Sheldon & Lawrence S. Krieger, *Understanding the Negative Effects of Legal Education on Law Students: A Longitudinal Test of Self-Determination Theory*, 33 Personality & Soc. Psychology Bull. 883 (2007).

classes or converting them entirely.[22] Most of us heard of these people during the shift in March 2020 to emergency remote teaching. With some time and space, they can help you make your course a more intentionally hybrid mix.[23] Some ideas an instructional designer may suggest are introduced and described in Chapter Six.

We Need More Hybrid Textbooks

The question of why the Kindle has not killed the printed book is an interesting one, and important for education at all levels. But the reasons are fairly obvious. First, because some types of written information work well in electronic form and others do not, and second, because human beings read in different ways. While it might take extra effort to drive to a bookstore to purchase a book, sometimes we want to browse, and sit with other readers. Books are a 500-year-old technology, one impossible to improve upon. The Kindle is wonderful in many ways, but is a poor medium for instructional manuals, travel guides, or cookbooks. On the other hand, if you enjoy serialized novels, finish one and want the next one, then you can get it on your Kindle in 60 seconds, which is a terrific convenience.

In legal education, the fact that we are still sending our students to the bookstore to spend $200 on a collection of cases that have been free online for a decade is a dinosaur waiting to die. Sure, there are interstitial materials between the cases in these books, and the cases are edited, but is the value of that great enough to justify putting an additional cost burden on our students of approximately $1,000 per semester? It might be—if there were no alternatives. But it is not, because there are alternatives.

We have had two catalogs of high-quality online casebooks for many years: the eLangdell collection,[24] sponsored and hosted by the Center for Computer-Aided Legal Instruction (CALI), and the H2O Project,[25] hosted by Harvard Law School. Each has a catalog of in excess of fifty casebooks covering every

22. Elaine Beirne & Matthew P. Romanoski, *Instructional Design in Higher Education: Defining an Evolving Field*, Online Learning Consortium Rsch. Ctr. Digit. Learning & Leadership (July 2018), http://olc-wordpress-assets.s3.amazonaws.com/uploads/2018/07/Instructional-Design-in-Higher-Education-Defining-an-Evolving-Field.pdf.

23. *Id.*

24. For more information, *see* https://www.cali.org/the-elangdell-bookstore.

25. For more information, *see* https://h2o.law.harvard.edu/.

major doctrinal subject in law school. They are either free, or substantially cheaper than the print books.[26]

It is interesting that these fully online textbooks have had limited success. Perhaps this is because it is different and requires a professor retooling their teaching to a different text in a different format. Or maybe it is because a fully online text does not work for all that students need to do with it, but a hybrid casebook would.

The future of law school teaching materials will depend on striking the balance between what students need in print, and then selecting the right things to make available online to go with it. The goal is to provide just enough in print to lay the proper groundwork, and no more. The sweet spot lives somewhere in that balance. Just as we need more hybrid teaching, we need hybrid textbooks to support it. Many legal book publishers in the last ten years have tried all manner of combinations to find the answer to the future of book publishing. A traditional print text with an exact copy of it in some form of online reader software—many have tried that. The online version of their books may have links into their online research database, but other than that, the two are the same, and no effort was made to select what is best in print and what is best online. Another publisher tried an entirely online book that struggled, and then changed direction and had all the online content printed in a 550-page book. Neither approach caught on. We have several efforts underway to create "crowdsourced" books that live fully online, but these mostly follow the standard format of the traditional casebook.

The reality is that students like print.[27] After all, it is a 570-year-old technology and it works well for certain kinds of reading and retention. There are a few textbook series that have tried to hit this hybrid mix properly,[28] although they are rare, and professors do not seem to understand what they are yet. But what is most lacking about these various attempts is, with a few exceptions,

26. *Guide: Creating an Account*, H20 Project, https://h2o.law.harvard.edu/p/create_account_help (last visited Sept. 1, 2022); Ctr. Computer-Assisted Legal Instruction, https://www.cali.org/the-elangdell-bookstore (last visited Sept. 1, 2022).

27. Michael Shaub, *92% of College Students Prefer Print Books to E-books*, Study Finds, LA Times (Feb. 8, 2016, 10:28 AM PT), https://www.latimes.com/books/jacketcopy/la-et-jc-92-percent-college-students-prefer-paper-over-pixels-20160208-story.html.

28. Among these are the Skills & Values Series, published by Carolina Academic Press. For more information, *see* https://cap-press.com/ms/257/Skills-&-Values-Series. West Publishing has developed the Doctrine and Practice Series, which also follows a hybrid model. *See* https://www.westacademic.com/series/Doctrine-and-Practice-Series.

little effort is being made to create truly new forms of teaching materials, much less to do the hard work of selecting what is best for print, and what is best for online. We need to make these choices in our hybrid courses, and then demand teaching materials from the publishers that support this mixed modality of teaching.

The co-founder of Apple Computer, Steve Jobs, was *insistent* that Apple's products be "edited products," and he repeatedly forced his engineers to consciously leave things out.[29] He wanted Apple products to be simple and elegant. The great jazz musician Charlie Mingus said: "Making the simple complicated is commonplace; making the complicated simple, awesomely simple, that's creativity."[30] The law is certainly complicated, but there is much more we could do to make it simpler and easier for students to learn.

Conclusion

Today, we are living hybrid lives and this flexible mix of in-person and online work is already becoming the standard in the legal profession and the courts. So it only makes sense that the lessons we have learned about hybrid online instruction should be expanded in the future of legal education. It is how our students are living, and it is how they will practice, so legal education should reflect that.

Doing so will also allow us to embrace a new model for legal education, where we admit a larger cohort at a lower cost for a hybrid first year of law school. There is early research that it would create a more egalitarian learning and participatory environment for BIPOC students, and this should help us improve the professional identity formation issues that some of those students experience in law school.

It is not possible to say what the ideal mix of online and in-person instruction is for each course, for each level of law school. But there is an incredibly interesting conversation we need to be having about those questions, and as law professors always do, we will share what we have learned, and legal education will improve as a result. It seems likely that we need to learn to redesign

29. Steve Lohr, *Steve Jobs and the Economics of Elitism*, NY Times (Jan. 30, 2010), www.nytimes.com/2010/01/31/weekinreview/31lohr.html.

30. *Parting Words: Charles Mingus*, All Things Considered, NPR (July 27, 2008, 4:00 PM ET) available at https://www.npr.org/2008/07/27/92976018/parting-words-charles-mingus.

our courses, and to create learning materials that are less tied to the old style of casebook learning. None of this will happen overnight, but much of it is happening already. For example, small experiments and part-time student programs are underway in numerous law schools around the country.

In short, we need to use the pandemic as an opportunity to reflect on the shortcomings of what we had before, and to build a new format for legal educational that is redefined by being more nimble, welcoming of difference, and hybridized, all of which will better prepare our students for their future, not our past.

SIX

Online Learning Is Part of Our Future

Introduction

This book has argued that the way to make legal education more relevant to the practice of law of today and of the future is to expand experiential learning opportunities in law school. But the cost of legal education is already high. So, this book also argues that we need to reduce the cost of legal education and at the same time increase its value and relevance. And it argues that we must dispense with the LSAT and break down traditional barriers to law school. These three goals seem opposite to each other, and can indeed conflict.[1]

This chapter describes in greater detail how these goals can all be pursued simultaneously: by moving more of the foundational first year courses to a hybrid online environment and admitting a larger cohort of law students. There are many topics in law school that law students can effectively learn online and doing so would reduce the cost substantially, as well as be more consistent with the hybrid future. It would also make available teaching resources for more hybrid experiential learning courses in the second and third years of law school.

1. Portions of this chapter were originally published in David I. C. Thomson, *How Online Learning Can Help Address Three Persistent Problems in Legal Education*, 70 Syracuse L. Rev. 181 (2020), and in David I. C. Thomson, *How Online Learning Will Transform Legal Education*, *in* Research Handbook on Digital Transformations, (F. Xavier Olleros and Majlinda Zhegu eds. Elgar 2016), and are reprinted here with permission.

Teaching Law Online

The debate about whether we should teach law online is over. Indeed, it has been over for some time, but the Covid pandemic proved to many skeptics that this can work. Today the tools, disciplines, and practices of online learning pervade law school courses, whether nominally taught online or not. Whether through Zoom, a website that offers quizzes on legal subjects, or through a full-featured learning management system which hosts links to myriad supplemental materials for the course, law professors are regularly using interactive and engaging online learning tools to enhance their courses.[2] Only a few years ago we could not imagine it, but it is commonplace now.

And it turns out that—even after the considerable disruption in teaching modalities created by the pandemic—students do not mind online modalities for their learning in law school and some want more. The ABA recently published the results of a survey conducted of 3L students graduating in 2022. When asked, "If a return to in-person learning was permitted by your law school for the current academic year, did you choose to enroll in any distance education courses this academic year?" A majority of students (57.47 percent) said yes, while 42.53 percent said no. While that is not an overwhelming preference, it still indicates that students want to take such courses. When the survey asked, "If you had a choice to take a course in-person or through Zoom or other web broadcast where all students are remote, which format would you prefer," 52.29 percent of students responded in favor of Zoom. Even more revealing was the answer to the question, "Do you want the ability to earn more distance education course credit than your law school currently allows?" For that question, 68.65 percent said yes. Finally, the survey asked, "Should the [ABA] Standards differentiate between credit hours earned through asynchronous, as opposed to synchronous, distance education courses," to which 76 percent of respondents said no.[3]

---

2. *See, e.g.*, *Resources for TWEN*, Thomson Reuters, https://lawschool.westlaw.com/marketing/display/si/1 (last visited Nov. 10, 2019); *Main Menu*, Ctr. for Comput. Assisted Legal Educ. (CALI), https://www.cali.org/ (last visited Nov. 10, 2021).

3. A.B.A. Comm. on Legal Educ. and Admissions to the Bar, *Distance Education Survey: 3L Student Quantitative Responses*, July 2022, https://www.americanbar.org/content/dam/aba/administrative/legal_education_and_admissions_to_the_bar/2022/22-distance-ed-survey-responses.pdf; *See also*, Jacquelyn Petzold et. al., *Success with Online Education*, October 2022, (Reporting on a survey of 13,000 law students at 70 schools indicating that over 75% of students are comfortable with nearly all aspects of attending online classes), Law School Survey of Student Engagement, 2022 Annual Survey Results, Oct. 2022, https://lssse

During the pandemic we learned that law professors can adapt. In a two-year study conducted by AccessLex and Gallup, students noted that at first—during the emergency remote teaching of the spring of 2020—there was a perceived gap between online and in-person instruction in law school, that gap narrowed the following year.[4] In 2021, 51 percent of law students taking at least half their classes online rated their programs as "Excellent" or "Good," while in 2022, 73 percent of hybrid and completely online students rated their programs as "Excellent" or "Good."[5] Further, the study found that 51 percent of 2021 students in mostly or completely face to face programs agreed that "their professors were using teaching methods that engaged them."[6] In 2022 that percentage increased to 60 percent, indicating that law students now "perceive a narrower gap between online, hybrid and in-person learning."[7]

Of course, distance education has a long history that goes back as far as the correspondence schools that sprung up during the middle of the nineteenth century. In the last forty years, as technologies more advanced than the paper mail system came online, distance educators adopted whatever new technology they could, and distance education grew. From the Pony Express to "snail" mail to bulletin boards to email to the web, distance education has been generally opportunistic and platform neutral. However, it was only in the last decade or so that the available technology allowed for a range of instructional modalities to support out-of-class and hybrid instruction, and the speed and ubiquity of broadband connection became reliable and fast enough to support it.

With the advent of the high-speed and mobile web, numerous technologies became available that support a level and quality of online instruction that was not previously possible. Enterprising teachers throughout the world have taken to these technologies and made them a part of their research as well as their instruction. One of these is Paul Maharg, retired professor of legal education at the University of Northern Australia. He has pioneered the use

.indiana.edu/wp-content/uploads/2022/10/Success-with-Online-Education-Final-10.26.22.pdf.

4. *Law School in a Pandemic: Student Perspectives on Distance Education and Lessons for the Future* (June 16, 2021) (Gallup/AccessLex) https://www.gallup.com/analytics/350876/accesslex-law-student-outcomes.aspx.

5. *Id.*

6. Susan D'Agostino, *Gap Between Online and In-Person Learning Narrows*. Inside Higher Ed. (July 13, 2022) https://www.insidehighered.com/news/2022/07/13/law-school-gaps-between-online-and-person-learning-narrow.

7. *Id.*

of virtual worlds for students to interact with in a skills-based simulation over the length of a semester or course.[8] He also has pioneered the concept of the "standardized client" in which a series of paid assistants play the "client" to a set script and set of facts—either live or online—and are reviewed for consistency and accuracy. The standardized client helps to equalize the work being asked of students in online classes with their counterparts in the same "ground" class and this also helps with uniform assessment methods.

Given the rise in the cost of law school, the job market for many of our graduates, and the need for law schools to produce "practice-ready" graduates, a common panacea offered is that law school should be shortened to two years by cutting off the third year, thus reducing the cost by a third.[9] No less than the former President of the United States Barack Obama—a graduate of Harvard Law and a former law professor at Chicago Law—has made the same suggestion.[10] Proponents of such proposals never seem to explain how the need for practice-ready graduates can be reconciled with removing the year in which students begin the transition into practice and generally receive the experiential opportunities to help them get ready for practice, through clinics, intensive simulations, and externship opportunities. We find ourselves again in the middle of a seemingly unresolvable conflict between needing to reduce the cost of law school and yet providing better and costlier learning opportunities.

Law schools could certainly make better use of the third year, but as this book has described, the ways the last year of law school are being used today have evolved substantially in the last 20 years. Now most law schools make available to students—particularly in the third year—experiential (practice-based) learning, either through simulation-based courses, clinics, or supervised externships. At this point, removing the third year would push us backward in meeting the educational needs of our students and properly preparing them for the more challenging market they are about to enter.

However, one of the reasons the idea to reduce law school to two years is so attractive to many pundits is that it would—emphatically and in one stroke—reduce the cost by a third. But it would also reduce preparedness for practice, and no one wants poorly prepared lawyers.

---

8. Karen Barton et al., *Simshare: Open Educational Resources in Simulation Learning* (BILETA Annual Conference 2010).

9. Daniel B. Rodriguez & Samuel Estreicher, *Make Law School Earn a Third Year*, N.Y. Times, Jan. 17, 2013, at A27.

10. Peter Lattman, *Obama says Law School Should be Two, Not Three, Years*, N.Y. Times, Aug. 24, 2013, at B3.

This chapter argues that a likely resolution to this conundrum is the "reduction" of law school to two years, accomplished in the opposite way: by removing the *first year* as we traditionally think of it. Or more specifically, significantly *reengineering* it, by putting most of it online and reducing the cost. The day when well-designed online learning environments began to achieve outcomes equivalent to or better than "ground" classes has long since passed. The first year classes mostly involve information transfer, and thus are ideally suited to hybrid online pedagogy. There is every reason to think there are acceptable ways to teach much of the first year material primarily online.

And not just acceptable ways—if constructed and executed well, online courses can deliver *better* learning outcomes than the current large class model for most first year courses in their traditional format.[11] Accepting this requires an understanding of what is currently happening in those large classes. While some of them are good and effective, some of them are not especially effective. The student who is engaged in dialog with the professor benefits, but the other students are merely watching, and often are distracted by what is on their laptops. The way the student "on call" thinks about a particular problem may not be the way another student thinks about it, and as a result, it is hard for the second student to follow the discussion. It is, in short, the opposite of one-on-one instruction, where the professor is able to individually "meet" the student where they are.

The use of technology outside of class can help law professors teach better (and students to learn better) when there is class time together.[12] As Harvard Law Professor Lael Weinberger writes:

> Using well-written, computer assisted instruction, students can be drilled and required to demonstrate the mastery of the black-letter law before they come to class. Then the limited classroom time can be used more effectively, as students more confidently engage in the face-to-face interaction with an expert in the subject area. . . .[13]

---

11. *See generally,* Working Group on Distance Learning in Legal Education, Distance Learning in Legal Education: Design, Delivery, and Recommended Practices (CALI, 2017).

12. Barry R. Vickrey, *The Changing Practice of Law and Law Schools: Why Would Anyone Go to Law School Today*, 60 S.D.L. Rev. 79, 89 (2015).

13. *Id.* at 90; *see also* Lael Weinberger, *Keep Distance Education for Law Schools: Online Education, the Pandemic, and Access to Justice*, 53 Loy. Chi. U. L.J. 211 (2021).

Delivering first year doctrinal instruction online in no way precludes the possibility of some hybrid teaching. That is, while students are taking the first year coursework online, they could be attending occasional Saturday classes where the Socratic method is employed.

So, for substantially reduced cost, law schools could then allow more students to enter the first year online, to study the basic first year courses—Civil Procedure, Criminal Law, Contracts, Property, and Torts—at their own pace over the period of a year or even two. Typically, they would be working during this period and thus would not lose the opportunity cost currently forfeited while in the first year of law school, where students are allowed to work outside of school only in limited circumstances. Students complete the "first" year when they pass their competency exams for each course. Not everyone would pass, but this would allow for an admissions process based more on suitability for law study than on prior privilege.

Online Learning Can Help Us Dispense With the LSAT

One of the central arguments of this book is that we must dispense with the LSAT as a barrier, making law school more accessible for minority students in one stroke. Instead of being judged on their LSAT score—a test that has little relationship to what lawyers do—students in the online first year would be judged on how well they learned what lawyers need to know. If some students never advanced, they would have paid a lower cost for a basic understanding of how the law operates, which would be a public good in itself, broadening the public's understanding of how our democratic institutions function. A Master's in American Law could be offered, and it might be all those students want or need. Offering such a degree would serve to provide value in exchange for tuition provided and time expended, something students who only go through the first year of law school currently do not have. Further, it would increase the value of the J.D. by distinguishing it from the first year degree.

If a student wanted to obtain the J.D. and did well enough in the first year to be admitted, the "second" year would include the remaining core courses in the first semester (such as Professional Responsibility, Constitutional Law, Evidence, and Administrative Law), and then transition to more simulation-based experiential learning in the spring semester, including training in legal research, writing, and advocacy. This year would be the first that students were primarily on campus, and in which they would leave their jobs behind.

"Third" year would continue with more experiential learning and add a supervised externship or a clinic.

Law schools adopting such a model could receive the same tuition revenue they currently receive by admitting more students,[14] and there would be room for them, since the "first" year students would not be in the law school building, or only at limited times. While some law schools have been criticized for graduating too many into a saturated market, if they were able to practice on day one—and their debt was not so burdensome—they could help to address another perennial problem: the large numbers of individuals and businesses who need a lawyer but cannot afford one, as documented in a study conducted by the Institute for the Advancement of the American Legal System.[15]

Perhaps most importantly, the best work that law schools have always done has been in the "high-touch" work that law professors do in the upper-class courses, and less often in the large lectures to 90 students at a time that are common in the first year. Instead of reducing the valuable learning time and attention that takes place in the second and third year, we should keep it, and move the fairly routine and basic work of the first year into an environment that is known to work well, is much cheaper, and that will provide a more egalitarian form of access to legal training that is based on suitability to the work that lawyers do.

So, if for reasons of cost and expediency, we need to get "rid" of a year of law school, it should be the *first year*, not the third. Or rather, we should reengineer law school by transferring those parts of it that are fairly rote forms of information transfer—including parts of the first year—to a well-designed hybrid online learning program with appropriate forms of assessment to measure learning and improve the redesigned program of instruction.

The First Year Course Content

Most of what is taught in the first year of law school is heavily content-based. It is focused on the foundational topics of the law: Contracts, Torts, Property, Civil Procedure, and Criminal Law. Each of these topics has a struc-

14. While the finances of each law school differ, an example financial model explaining and supporting this proposal as applied to six diverse schools is provided in Chapter Eight.

15. Natalie Anne Knowlton, *Cases Without Counsel: Our Recommendations After Listening to Litigants*, Inst. for the Advancement of the Am. Legal Sys. (IAALS) (2016) available at https://iaals.du.edu/sites/default/files/documents/publications/cases_without_counsel_recommendations_report.pdf.

ture, method, and key principles that every law student needs to learn. In the dominant teaching method, students typically read cases for each class, which have embedded in them the rules and principles of law. Class time is often spent in a combination of a professor's lecture—interspersed with dialog with a student—about what each case illustrates. Over the course of the semester, all the students in the class are supposed to determine the structure and principles embedded in the cases and prepare for a final exam, which often determines all (or most) of their grade for the course.

It is certainly true that one professor teaching a large number of students is economically efficient, but it was a model designed for efficiency and tuition revenue, not necessarily as an ideal model for learning. During a typical class, if one student is the only one on "call," all the other students are in a passive mode, listening. This is a particularly good example of time spent in class that could be replicated online. In that case, the other students are already "watching" what is going on—they are just watching it in a video stream, rather than in the classroom with the student being questioned. After the class has concluded, a taped video has an additional advantage: the student can start and stop the tape and review as they go through it, which is obviously impossible to do in a live class.

It is also certainly true that students learn a lot from each other. That is, in between classes, when they review together concepts they learned in class, this is a helpful—although informal—element of their learning. If they are members of a disciplined study group, this can be even more supportive of their learning. But today, with the application of widely available (and regularly used) technology, none of that sort of 1L learning *needs* to happen in the same physical space. This generation of students is adept—indeed fluent—in the ability to keep in contact with, and learn from, people they mostly know through the numerous social apps that they use on their phones.

Online learning works,[16] and it can be an effective delivery system for much of the content that is contained in the 1L courses. Moving the 1L year online, particularly if it has some hybrid components and technology-assisted community building, should be successful.

16. Doug Lederman, *Online Education Ascends*, Inside Higher Ed (November 7, 2018), https://www.insidehighered.com/digital-learning/article/2018/11/07/new-data-online-enrollments-grow-and-share-overall-enrollment; *see also* Tan Nguyen, *The Effectiveness of Online Learning: Beyond No Significant Difference and Future Horizons*, 11 MERLOT J. Online Learning and Teaching 309, 310–12 (2015).

A Proposed Model Curriculum

With these concepts in mind, this is what a hybrid (but heavily online) first year curriculum could look like.

First Year of Law School

10 credits online, 18 total, low residency

FALL SEMESTER

Torts *(4 online credits)*
15/85 (hybrid ratio—in person/online)

Contracts *(4 non-online credits)*
67/33 (hybrid ratio—in person/online)

Intro to Legal Writing I *(1 online credit)*
15/85 (hybrid ratio—in person/online)

SPRING SEMESTER

Property *(4 online credits)*
15/85 (hybrid ratio–in person/online)

Civil Procedure *(4 non-online credits)*
67/33 (hybrid ratio—in person/online)

Intro to Legal Writing II *(1 online credit)*
15/85 (hybrid ratio—in person/online)

At the end of each semester, students would have to pass rigorous examinations in the doctrinal courses and take a writing test—much like the bar examination's "performance test"—and pass that as well. This exam could be very much like, and draw on the experience with, the "Baby Bar" that is commonly administered in California state accredited law schools.[17] In this model, somewhat more than half of the cohort would pass these tests, but

17. For more information on the California First Year Law Student Exam, *see* https://www.calbar.ca.gov/Admissions/Examinations/First-Year-Law-Students-Examination/First-Year-Exam-Grading-and-Scope

those that did not—but did well enough to deserve it—would be awarded a Master's in American Law (of some sort), which for some professionals might be all they need.[18] Further, this degree could become one of the qualifications for further study to become a Limited License Legal Practitioner ("LLLT"). There are different versions of LLLT programs across the country, all designed with the goal of increasing access to justice. Some states, such as New York and Utah, have found success with these types of program, and several states, including Colorado and Arizona, are in the preliminary stages of incorporating an LLLT program into their state's legal practice.[19] But it seems likely that, as LLLT opportunities spread across the country, some students would come to law school only with the intention of doing that work, and this would help to address the access to justice gap. They would be able to do that work because they would have significantly less debt, having taken a year at a reduced cost in this model, and not continued for two more years. Those that pass the first year "bar exam" would be admitted to what we traditionally think of as second year of law school.

In the second year, students would take fifteen credits of hybrid online instruction, and their curriculum could look like this:

18. So, the "baby bar" would have a High Pass—admission to 2L in law school for the J.D.—and a Low Pass—which would award the Master's degree. It is not assumed that any score, even a very low one, would still be awarded the Master's degree.

19. *See, e.g.*, Shelly Bradbury, *Non-Attorneys Practicing Law? Colorado Eyes New Legal License for Divorce, Child Custody Cases*, https://www.denverpost.com/2022/08/07/colorado-licensed-legal-paraprofessional-family-law/; Avery Martinez, *What's the Future for Limited Liability Legal Technicians?*, Law Week Colo. (Sept. 10, 2020), https://www.lawweekcolorado.com/article/lllt-programs/; *see generally*, Mary E. McClymont, *Nonlawyer Navigators in State Courts: An Emerging Consensus*, Just. Lab at Geo. L., 9–11 (June 2019), https://www.ncsc.org/__data/assets/pdf_file/0024/53691/Justice-Lab-Navigator-Report-6.11.19.pdf; Patrick McGlone, *Can Licensed Legal Paraprofessionals Narrow the Access-to-justice Gap?*, A.B.A. J. (Sept. 6, 2018), http://www.abajournal.com/news/article/can_licensed_legal_paraprofessionals_narrow_the_access_to_justice_gap; Catherine J. Dupont, *Licensed Paralegal Practitioners*, 31 Utah Bar J. 40 (2018); Debra Cassens Weiss, *First Paralegal Practitioners in Utah are Expected to be Licensed in 2019*, A.B.A. J. (Aug, 7, 2018), http://www.abajournal.com/news/article/first_paralegal_practitioners_in_utah_are_expected_to_be_licensed_in_2019; *Licensed Paralegal Practitioner Program*, Utah St. Bar, https://www.utahbar.org/licensed-paralegal-practitioner/ (last visited Aug. 21, 2022).

Second Year of Law School

Providing 15 credits online, and a transition year to reduce outside work, with greater in-residence at the law school:

FALL SEMESTER

Constitutional Law *(4 online credits)*
15/85 (hybrid ratio–in person/online)

Administrative Law *(3 online credits)*
15/85 (hybrid ratio–in person/online)

Lawyering Process I *(3 in-person credits)*
67/33 (hybrid ratio–in person/online)

SPRING SEMESTER

Criminal Law *(4 online credits)*
15/85 (hybrid ratio–in person/online)

Evidence *(4 online credits)*
15/85 (hybrid ratio–in person/online)

Lawyering Process II *(3 in-person credits)*
67/33 (hybrid ratio–in person/online)

The types of courses contemplated in this (example) course design, with a 15/85 hybrid ratio, can be delivered—at least in part—in what is known as the "flipped classroom" format. In this course design, much of the "content" of the course is delivered in an online (whether asynchronous, synchronous, or a mix of both) format, and the in-person class time is used to leverage that information in a more interactive format.

If a student were to take four years to finish the degree, they would stay with this sort of 2L year, and might again be able to keep their jobs and attend law school in the evenings or on weekends. If they were going to take three years to finish the degree, they would need to take an additional course or clinic each semester in the 2L year. And because the first year was "light" on credits (at least compared to what first year students currently take), they would need to take six credits to catch up in the summer after their 2L year. Of course, many students—particularly part-time students—take summer courses for similar reasons already.

At this point, if the student were taking four years to complete the degree, they would have thirty-nine credits completed, but if they were taking three years, they would have fifty-one credits completed, and have thirty-nine to go. That would, admittedly, leave a heavy 3L year of 19.5 credits per semester, but with externship and semester-in-practice programs that are becoming common in law schools today, this is possible.

For the remainder of their time in law school—however the time was allocated—students would still have five credits left they could take in online courses. Legal Ethics is one of the remaining required classes at all law schools, which would count for three additional online credits, since it could also be taught 15 percent in person and 85 percent online, and count as an online class. That leaves a two-credit online class—and there are many options in the curricula of most law schools that could be developed into a 15 percent in person and 85 percent online hybrid class format, such as Oil and Gas Law or Gender and the Law. Such a model would fulfill the total of thirty credits currently approved by the ABA to be provided online, but there should be no requirement that every student do that. After the first year, students should have the option—as the school's manpower allows—to take courses such as Legal Ethics in an online format or in a primarily in-person format.

But to achieve this model—or one like it—we will have to become better and more skilled at delivering hybrid online instruction. Law professors learned a lot about hybrid instruction during the pandemic, but there are some key principles that will help us to understand how to do this well as we move into our hybrid future.

Effective Online Pedagogy—We Can Do This

The first thing to understand about effective online teaching is that it is not about the technology involved.[20] It is tempting to think so, however. A law professor in 2020 might have said: "Just teach me how to do what I do online, and I'll go do that." This led to the "Zoom School of Law" problem early in the pandemic, and students tolerated it,[21] but are less likely to do so as they

---

20. Portions of this chapter were originally published in David I. C. Thomson, *Elements of Effective Online Instruction in Law*, 65 St. Louis U. L.J. 703 (2021), and are reprinted here with permission.

21. *Law School in Pandemic, Year 2—Moving from Emergency Remote Teaching to Emerging Best Practices in Distance Legal Education*, Gallup & AccessLex Inst., 7–13 (2022),

themselves come to understand what an effective online learning environment is and is not. This is because good online course pedagogy requires rethinking and redesigning each course from back to front.

Yes, back first. Because it is time—overdue according to the ABA's accreditation requirement[22]—to articulate the measurable learning outcomes for each course that we offer in our law schools. If we start with the end in mind, we will have a much better idea of how to redesign the course as a whole. It seems like a tedious exercise, but as an expert in this subject, it should not take each law professor more than half an hour.

The magic happens when you have that list.[23] Because then you can divide the individual outcomes by the amount of time you have, and apportion it to each outcome, and then think about how to measure whether your students have achieved that learning outcome while the course is progressing. And that leads to multiple assessments, preferably ones that are "formative"[24] or encourage learning through the course, not just measure it at the end—such as the all-in final exam that is still so common in law schools. Also, when you have articulated your list of learning outcomes, you can share it with your students. This helps them to understand what you are teaching them, and what these formative assessments are for. They will have a better understanding of how they are doing during the course and have the opportunity to correct their trajectory before it is too late.

What this all leads to is a fundamentally different approach to course design. In this approach, you decide what the outcomes are, and then you

---

https://www.accesslex.org/law-school-in-a-pandemic-year-2. *See also* Kathryn Hobbis, *Zoom School of Law?*, 34 Geo. J. Legal Ethics 1025, 1025 (2021); Lucy I. Johnston-Walsh & Alison Lintal, *Tele-Lawyering and the Virtual Learning Experience: Finding the Silver Lining for Remote Hybrid Externships & Law Clinics after the Pandemic*, 54 Akron L. Rev. 735, 743 (2021).

22. A.B.A. Section of Legal Educ. & Admissions to the Bar, *ABA Standards and Rules of Procedure for Approval of Law Schools 2020–2021*, Standard 314 (2020), available at https://www.americanbar.org/content/dam/aba/administrative/legal_education_and_admissions_to_the_bar/standards/2020-2021/2020-21-aba-standards-and-rules-chapter3.pdf [hereafter A.B.A. Standards 2020–2021].

23. *See Getting Started with Writing Learning Outcomes*, Cornell Univ. Ctr. for Teaching Innovation, https://teaching.cornell.edu/resource/getting-started-writing-learning-outcomes (last visited Aug. 21, 2022).

24. *What is the Difference Between Formative and Summative Assessment?*, Carnegie Mellon Univ. Eberly Ctr., https://www.cmu.edu/teaching/assessment/basics/formative-summative.html (last visited Aug. 21, 2022). More information about law school assessment is provided in Chapter Two.

divide the material into digestible components and place them into an order that makes clear to students what they are learning and why. Each step, or component, of the newly designed syllabus has an optimal length of time assigned to it, and a companion assessment. When this "chunking" of the syllabus is complete, the transition to hybrid online instruction can take place.

Because then—and only then—should the professor select the learning activity that will best deliver the learning objective. Will it be an asynchronous lecture component on that topic, with an embedded quiz? Will it be a short (synchronous) live lecture on the topic, with some group work? The professor should select the assignment or activity to meet the learning goal, which means that the online modalities will vary throughout the semester.[25] To suggest that you should make live (synchronous) teaching the "default"[26] with tape available to students who could not be "there" (whether in person or online at the particular time you offered it) is to lose the opportunity to leverage the best teaching technology to optimally meet the learning outcome you have identified. Put another way, if a course design uses all the same modality (for example: live lecture on Zoom or all asynchronous lectures, etc.) then you have a pretty good idea that it was not redesigned from the back to the front. And it is likely not using the optimal activity and technology to meet each of the myriad learning outcomes for the course. It is, unfortunately, trying to replicate the traditional classroom experience with one teaching modality, and squandering the opportunity that online learning affords us to teach in a more effective multi-modal manner.

Online Learning and Assessment

There is a silver lining in the expanded use of online learning technologies that we are currently experiencing. It is possible to automate much of this, and to have the upfront work reusable each year thereafter. Online quizzes are the most obvious form of this, but there are ways to embed assessment in video, and of course you can have a discussion board that teaching assistants can review. Many of these already exist,[27] and many legal textbook authors

---

25. See David Sandomierski & Stephanie Ben-Ishai, *Modular Legal Learning: Revitalizing the Law Classroom*, 45 Dal. L. J. 2, 8–9 (2022) (setting out five principles that should guide efforts to integrate synchronous modules into legal education).

26. Nina A. Kohn, *Teaching Law Online: A Guide for Faculty*, (forthcoming 2020) (manuscript at 4–6), available at https://papers.ssrn.com/sol3/papers.cfm?abstract_id=3648536.

27. A complete listing of the several hundred currently available CALI Lessons can be found here: *Lessons*, CALI, https://www.cali.org/lesson (last visited Aug. 21, 2022).

have developed similar assessments. Research has shown that students need not only just the one quiz near the time they learned the concept but also follow-up questions about the concepts so they retain what they learned over time. This is known as "spaced repetition,"[28] and these assessment formats are both available for the major subjects and customizable by the professor. There are short-answer questions that might generate a paragraph of text, but these can be peer-reviewed by the students for each other with some upfront training and (reusable) effort.[29]

If each component of the course had a quiz or self- or peer-assessment at the end, students would benefit and much research indicates their learning would improve.[30] It is certainly still acceptable to retain the final exam at the end of the course (the "summative assessment") but it can carry less grade weight than it did previously. This way, the formative assessments throughout the course have some grade incentive, and the students have an idea of how they are doing before they get to the final exam. Because these types of assessments are fairly easy to create and administer in the online environment, and reusable year after year, you will find that students will appreciate them, their final exams will be better, and—best of all—the ABA will approve.[31]

Benefits of Hybrid Course Design

During the initial phase of the Covid crisis, most law schools shifted their courses to a fully online teaching environment.[32] Some of them continued this practice in the fall semester of 2020.[33] While fully online courses can work and be effective—with at least the work contemplated above and in Chapter Two

28. For information about Spaced Repetition as a learning methodology, and the SeRiouS™ software for law students that uses it, *see* Spaced Repetition, http://www spaced repetition.com (last visited Aug. 21, 2022).

29. *See* Tracy Leigh McKinzie Norton, *Peerceptiv Student Intro 5: Back Evaluations*, YouTube (Aug. 21, 2017), https://www.youtube.com/watch?v=BRjTiW-oHII&t=7s.

30. Sean H. K. Kang, *Spaced Repetition Promotes Efficient and Effective Learning: Policy Implications for Instruction*, 3 Pol'y Insights Behav. & Brain Scis. 12, 13 (2015).

31. A.B.A. Standards 2020–2021, *supra* note 22, at Standard 314.

32. Karen Sloan, *Here Are the Law Schools Moving Classes Online Amid Coronavirus*, Law.com (Mar. 10, 2020, 2:05 PM), https://www.law.com/2020/03/10/here-are-the-law-schools-moving-classes-online-amid-coronavirus/.

33. Karen Sloan, *Law Schools that Planned to Return to Campus in Fall are Reversing Course*, Law.com (Aug. 5, 2020, 2:21 PM), https://www.law.com/nationallawjournal/2020/08/05/law-schools-that-planned-to-return-to-campus-in-fall-are-reversing-course/.

being completed and improved year after year—some of what we do seems more effective in an in-person environment. Zoom is terrific for many group discussions, but nuances of expression are hard to pick up on—both ways—in the "Brady Bunch" screen, and in larger classes you cannot even see everyone at the same time. Clinical teaching relies on a lot of in-person interaction, and it is hard to have the experience of a courtroom (in, say, a Trial Practice class) in your bedroom. Many experiential courses—at their best—rely on some in-person learning.

So, what is needed in many cases is a hybrid learning environment that includes a mix of online and in-person instruction. One that leverages learning technologies to advance learning goals that can be effectively achieved online, and that maximizes the precious in-person time by reserving for those classes instruction and group work that can be most effectively delivered in that context. The *interesting* question is: what is it about each teaching modality that made it a better choice for a digital solution, and what is still better in an analog form? And the challenge is then to apply that test to the hybrid learning environment for every course.

It seems more than possible that not every moment spent in lecture in the traditional in-person classroom was optimized for that precious resource (the in-person time). It is possible that we took in-person class time for granted, professors and students alike. But we also noticed over the last decade (or more) that our students were occasionally tuning us out, and surfing on their laptops. This dreaded discovery led to some professors banning laptops[34] in their classrooms. An alternative response might be for us to look for those places where students were tuning out and selecting a teaching method that would engage them instead. A hybrid teaching environment can help us do this.

So, in addition to redesigning a course from back to front, and including assessments, the professor might spend some time thinking about whether the particular topic they are coming to next (say, the Mailbox Rule in Contracts) would be more effectively taught using a short video lecture with diagrams and followed by a quiz. That sounds difficult, but another great development of the last decade is that our law schools have terrific, and sadly often underutilized, tech staff members and instructional designers who can do much of this with instruction by the professor on the learning goal. Then, the precious in-person

---

34. Martha Neil, *More Law Profs Ban Laptop Use in Class,* A.B.A. J. (Jan. 12, 2010, 12:47 AM), https://www.abajournal.com/news/article/more_law_profs_bring_down_hammer_banning_laptop_use_in_class.

class time can be used to revisit, rediscover, and emphasize particular points or hypotheticals using, for example, the Mailbox Rule.

A hybrid learning environment is optimally designed with the maximization of the in-person time, as well as the utilization of the best technology to teach and embed a particular concept of law in our students. As we make these decisions in our courses, we will learn how to use the correct teaching modality in service of the planned learning goal for the particular course that we teach. And we will share this learning as it develops—in conferences and papers, as we always do.

The Importance of Clear and Regular Communication

Among the advantages of the traditional law classroom was that, for the most part, the expectations did not change. Read thirty pages. Come to class and we will talk about those cases. If we do not get to all of it, we will pick up where we left off in the next class. There will be a review session at the end, and one final exam for the full grade. This might not have been the best overall learning environment, but it did have the benefit of clear expectations.

In the more hybrid and multi-modal learning environment contemplated here, this advantage is exchanged for another. While the course materials and methods may be more complex than a strictly in-person class, adaptability to the needs of the learners will be improved. As noted, there are probably many "moving parts" to each component, and perhaps multiple modules for each part of the course. Students need to know where they have been, where they are, where they are going, and what is expected next. But in varying the modalities, the hybrid course design is more effective for a wider selection of students.

Fortunately, a lot of the complexity can be tamed by the learning management system (LMS), but it is important to do more than just that. It is recommended that you start each class with a reminder of where the course sits that day, and what is coming up. And this is true whether the class is in-person or in the form of an online component: at the end of an in-person class in week seven, for example, what is online and what needs to be completed before the next in-person class should be reiterated. Then, consider starting the next part of the asynchronous module online reiterating what was just covered in the in-person class, and what is coming up for this one. Yes, it all seems repetitive and perhaps tedious, but the hybrid environment requires it. And many students who might not be the best time managers will appreciate it.

Also, use email (of course). An introductory email to all students at the beginning of the course, and a check-in email every two or three weeks, is a good idea. Each LMS also has an announcement feature, which can be set up to generate an email to each enrolled student.

Selecting the best way to achieve each learning outcome is something easy to say, but not necessarily easy to do. We are still in the early days of broad deployment of these myriad tools and modalities, and it will take time before we really have developed best practices for each course and type of material being taught.[35] But each professor should enter into this with a spirit of inquiry and consider collecting data and learning as they go. Law professors are generally quite gifted teachers, and while the hybrid learning environment is challenging at first, it can also be intellectually engaging. Law professors like intellectual engagement, and they want to be good teachers. While much has yet to be investigated, there is a developing consensus on a few elements of this transition that should be helpful.

Asynchronous versus Synchronous Learning

This book has used the term "in-person" learning to refer to the traditional classroom environment, and it has made mention of asynchronous course content provided in the learning management system (LMS), where the professor might have taped a short lecture and added a quiz afterwards. Students are given a limited amount of time to complete that item of asynchronous course content before the next in-person class. But another option is synchronous online classes. This is where, during a set class time, everyone is together but online and is analogous to an in-person class. In the spring semester of 2020,

---

35. Fortunately, this is already underway. In the Summer of 2020, many sub-disciplines of law teaching held their own online conferences about effective online pedagogy. *See, e.g., William & Mary Conference for Excellence in Teaching Legal Research & Writing Online*, Wm. & Mary Conference for Excellence in Teaching Legal Research & Writing Online, Wm. & Mary L. Sch. (June 18–19, 2020), https://law.wm.edu/academics/intellectuallife/conferencesandlectures/excellence_online_teaching/index.php.

many faculty members used Zoom for this, with mixed results.[36] Some critics referred to it as "emergency remote teaching," not online pedagogy.[37]

But a live class on Zoom (or similar technology) has a function. If you need everyone to hear the same thing at the same time it works perfectly well. If you then need your students to act on that information in groups, live—well, then it is still a good option. Proceed to teach the content you need to but try to limit straight lecture to seven to ten minutes at a time.[38] Then use Zoom's breakout group feature and move from group to group, helping each group stay focused in their discussions. You want to be sure that you have given your students everything they need to succeed in the groups in advance. Perhaps that is where a companion asynchronous module would be beneficial. This course design is often referred to as the "flipped classroom"[39]—where much of the "content" is asynchronously provided, and the in-person time (whether in the classroom or on Zoom) is used to "process and apply" the content just learned. The important thing is to think through what the optimal "scaffolding"[40] of the material is for the majority of your students (it will never be perfect for all of them) and then design around those decisions. Simply putting everything online in synchronous live Zoom classes abdicates this work and the opportunity to be more effective and engaging with your students is lost.

An additional format is the "HyFlex" teaching environment. HyFlex is in-person teaching to some of your students, and remote teaching to others, at the same time—mediated by some sort of technology. (Thus the name: hybrid flexible, or HyFlex for short.) So it is hybrid primarily in the delivery

---

36. Kelsey J. Griffin, *Harvard Law Student Files Class Action Lawsuit Demanding Tuition Reimbursement*, Harv. Crimson (June 26, 2020), https://www.thecrimson.com/article/2020/6/26/harvard-coronavirus-law-school-tuition-lawsuit/; Marlyse Vieira, *Classes Online: Student Perspectives and Privacy Concerns about Zoom*, Va. L. Wkly. (Mar. 25, 2020), https://www.lawweekly.org/front-page/2020/3/25/classes-online-student-perspectives-and-privacy-concerns-about-zoom.

37. Charles Hodges et al., *The Difference Between Emergency Remote Teaching and Online Learning*, EducauseReview (Mar. 27, 2020), https://er.educause.edu/articles/2020/3/the-difference-between-emergency-remote-teaching-and-online-learning.

38. Philip J. Guo et al., *How Video Production Affects Student Engagement: An Empirical Study of MOOC Videos, Proc. ACM Conf. on Learning at Scale* (2014), https://dl.acm.org/doi/10.1145/2556325.2566239.

39. *See* William R. Slomanson, *Blended Learning: A Flipped Classroom Experiment*, 64 J. Legal Educ. 93, 95 (2014) (providing a description of the flipped learning model).

40. *See* Janneke van de Pol et al., *Scaffolding in Teacher-Student Interaction: A Decade of Research*, 22 Educ. Psych. Rev. 271, 273–77 (2010) for the concept of scaffolding in learning.

method, not the content. True hybrid teaching is in-person teaching to all of your students, with some online content—and perhaps occasional fully online (synchronous or asynchronous) classes for all students. These online classes and/or modules are purposefully added to enhance the teaching and learning taking place in the classroom.

HyFlex often requires a super-human effort by the teacher to bridge the in-person classroom with those at home, teaching essentially with two heads if you will. It can be done, but with no preparation during the pandemic, it was probably too much to ask our teachers to do with any regularity or expectation of simultaneous success in both spaces at once. Perhaps one day the technology will be better, and ubiquitous—with the bandwidth to support it—such that students in multiple places can be truly "present" in the classroom all at once. But for now, a hybrid approach is better.

General Online Teaching Tips

If you are not all able to be in-person for the first class, prepare a "class zero" at the beginning of your course. Post your syllabus well ahead of that class and make it a synchronous Zoom session. Spend some time getting to know your students, explain the syllabus and how the course will proceed. Send them into breakout groups so they can spend some time getting to know each other, using an ice-breaker you have designed. Meet your students' pets. Laugh. Encourage your students to connect with each other offline.

What we have learned so far is that law students—who already sought contact with their professors—crave it even more when learning from a distance. So anything you can do to create community and enhance contact with your students is encouraged. Virtual office hours, fully online on Zoom (or similar tools), have been popular with students.

Via email before that class zero, ask about accommodations that a student might need to fully participate in the class. We still have a digital divide, so make sure your students have sufficient bandwidth and camera and microphone. Arrange to get them tech help if they need it. Put them in touch with the dean of students for support, and point out that the accommodations office can also help. A little bit of outreach in this context can go a long way.

For live synchronous classes, use them more sparingly than usual, and take brief (five minute) breaks every twenty to thirty minutes. Allow students to use the chat function but ask them to limit their use to only public chat and assign a TA to monitor it for and with you. You can do random calling on students, or they can raise their hand or post a question in the chat.

Try to give students something to engage with regularly—every week at minimum. This could include online quizzes, small writing projects, and peer-review exercises. Simulation problems, involving a family member or fellow student acting as the client, can be effective. Virtual field trips—where a student might visit an online court hearing and report back to the class about what they learned—will be engaging. Using a streamed online court hearing—which are becoming increasingly available as courts have moved online—makes it so that all students can view the same court hearing wherever they are.

We all need to keep in mind that student well-being is critical to their success. This was always true, but it is particularly true in an online learning environment, where you will have fewer cues that a student is struggling. When you are teaching a live online class, ask all of your students to keep their video window on, and cycle through them during synchronous sessions so you can see them. Call on groups of students instead of individuals, to ease the pressure of performance anxiety, which for some can be heightened by the online environment. Use the extensive, and revealing, data that your LMS automatically compiles about student engagement with the material you post online.

Not All Content Fits in All Containers

When we design curricula, and individual courses, it is important to keep in mind that each component is not a widget. It does not necessarily fit every online context. The term "content" refers to what the teacher of any course will tell you what the generally accepted "content" for that course is (with their own preferences or modifications, which they can defend in detail). When a teacher says, "I have the following topics I need to cover in my course"—that is "content."

The term "container" refers to, in part, the class schedule. This is often expressed on a syllabus as something like this: "M/W 1:15–2:30; 3 Credits." For more than 100 years, we thought in terms of time and place-based containers. But the online teaching environment brought us many new forms of containers, such as synchronous, asynchronous, HyFlex, and hybrid teaching modalities. If part of the course content can be taught on an asynchronous schedule, the container takes on a very different dimension. So now "container" refers to the class schedule *and* the primary modality of instruction.

When we switched to online teaching, we made a big assumption—that all course content could be made to fit in any container. But this chapter argues the opposite of that assumption: *not* all content fits in all containers. There are some courses, by their content, that work best in person. Others work very well in a hybrid format. Others are completely suitable to well-designed asynchronous instruction formats—in whole. And the other side of this coin is that some course content does *not* fit well in some containers. So, we have to be intentional about course design and use the technological tool that best fits the particular component of content we are trying to teach.

Conclusion

The debate about whether we should teach law online is over. We need to open up law school to a broader, more diverse cohort of students. To do this, we need to redesign the first year of law school to be primarily online, with some hybrid components so students feel connected to their school and to their classmates.

While there is more we can learn together about how to design excellent online courses for the teaching of legal subjects, there is much we already know. We know that mixing modalities can work well to keep students engaged and to simulate legal practice. We know that technologies such as spaced repetition can help students learn, and that myriad assessment tools have advanced to support hybrid learning.

Reengineering the first year of law school, by rebuilding much of it online, is a critical component of the way forward for legal education. This would leave law faculties to do what most of them prefer to do and what they do best: teach students in smaller classes the more complex legal doctrine in the context of how it is used in practice, with a focus on what it will take to be an effective attorney in the twenty-first century.

SEVEN

We Must Reorient Law School Around the Preparation for Service

Introduction

In his 1993 classic book *The Lost Lawyer: Failing Ideals of the Legal Profession*, Anthony Kronman describes the ideal of the "lawyer-statesman," who is, ultimately, a devoted citizen.[1] In this conception, a lawyer "cares about the public good and is prepared to sacrifice [their] own well-being for it… this is a condition of being successful in [the] work."[2]

Not every law school has a mission statement, per se, on their website for all to see. But they all have an "About Our Law School" statement, often written (it seems) by marketing professionals. Of those schools that post a mission statement, few make mention of service to others. Most of these statements focus on words such as "empowering tomorrow's leaders,"[3] or equipping "students with knowledge and skills to ethically and effectively practice law and pursue justice."[4] A rare mention of service to others is found at the University of Colorado Law School's website, which uses this language: "… provides stu-

---

1. Anthony T. Kronman, The Lost Lawyer: Failing Ideals of the Legal Profession 14–15, 118–20 (Cambridge 1993).

2. *Id.* at 14–15.

3. *'Leading Social Change' Asks Students to Explore the 'One Big Thing' They Want to Change in the World*, Penn L., Univ. Pa. Carey Sch. L. (March 17, 2022), https://www.law.upenn.edu/live/news/14570-leading-social-change-asks-students-to-explore-the.

4. *The Future of Law*, Almanac, Wash. Univ. Sch. of L., https://www.brandalmanac.com/project/the-future-of-law/ (last visited Aug. 22, 2022).

dents with a state-of-the-art legal education and prepares them to serve wisely and with professionalism."[5] Columbia, a law school known for its corporate program and placements in the largest corporate law firms, uses this language: "our students complete their legal training ready to engage with the world's most challenging issues across borders, jurisdictions, subject matters, sectors, and industries."[6] The overall messaging on law school websites is primarily about efficacy. Our law school is worth your investment. It will pay off for you. But is that really what legal education is for, or should be for? Do those goals sufficiently prepare our graduates to sacrifice their own well-being for the public good?

Every state has its own oath of office that it asks all new attorneys who have passed the bar to take as part of a ceremony of admission to practice,[7] and each is different—some short, some long. The American Bar Association notes that every state's oath of admission has three requirements in common: (1) to uphold the United States Constitution, (2) to faithfully discharge the duties of an attorney, and (3) to conduct oneself with integrity and dignity.[8] Only fourteen states also include this language: "I will never reject from any consideration personal to myself the cause of the defenseless or oppressed."[9] Just three states also include a pledge that the newly minted attorney will "[s]trive to improve the law and the administration of justice,"[10] and Colorado adds to that: "I will use my knowledge of the law for the betterment of society."[11]

This mix of mission/about statements for law schools, and the mix of oaths of admission, indicates something about law schools and the legal profession. We have lost our way. This book argues that we have forgotten the central reason why law schools exist.

5. *About Colorado Law*, Colo. L., https://www.colorado.edu/law/about-colorado-law (last visited Aug. 22, 2022).

6. *About*, Colum. L. Sch., https://www.law.columbia.edu/about (last visited Aug. 22, 2022).

7. *Oaths of Admission for All 50 States*, https://cdn.ymaws.com/www.inbar.org/resource/resmgr/litigation/Oaths.pdf (compiled by Judge Margaret Robb of the Indiana Court of Appeals).

8. Robert Gottfried, *The Anatomy of Our Oath*, A.B.A., https://www.americanbar.org/groups/young_lawyers/publications/after-the-bar/professional-life/anatomy-of-our-oath/ (last visited Aug. 22, 2022).

9. One state, Kentucky, includes the requirement that the new attorney has never fought in a duel. *Id.*

10. *See supra* note 7.

11. Oath of Admission, Colo. Sup. Ct., Off. of Att'y Regul. Couns., https://coloradosupremecourt.com/Current%20Lawyers/Oath.asp (last visited Aug. 22, 2022).

The Goal of Legal Education Should Be Service

It is unfortunate, but much of legal education indexes the "value" of what it offers to a financial payoff. That is, if you can pay off your debt during your life as a lawyer, and make more money than that, then legal education offered a payoff for you.[12] It was "worth it." And as long as we have this as our lodestar, we will continue to bring in students seeking to enter, or stay in, the upper middle class. And we surely do need students, or we will have to turn the lights off. But we made a terrible mistake when we sold out to such a lowly goal, and the formation of professional identity—discussed in detail in Chapter Three—provides a clue for a better alternative.

We often in legal education explain that we teach our students to "think like a lawyer." Over time, we have discovered the limitations and imprecision of that goal. More recently, influenced by the *MacCrate Report* and the *Carnegie Report*, we have replaced that with a goal that our students be "practice-ready" or "prepared for practice" when they graduate. As in: the law school has provided value if our students pass the bar exam and are able to obtain and hold a legal job. There are doubts on both counts—some students do not pass the bar or feel underprepared for practice and have difficulty getting a job. But part of the problem is that this is the wrong orientation, and it has caused innumerable problems for legal education, as well as the profession it serves. We should be setting our sights higher, and instead we should be oriented around preparation for *service*.

Service should be our mantra and organizing principle—across law schools and in every state bar association. The practice of law is a service profession, not unlike those of doctors and clergy. We call ourselves a "profession" based in part on that service orientation. If legal education was oriented around service and the professional identity of a lawyer—not just the ethical rules, but more than that—we would be better off. And our students—and the profession and their future clients—would be also. The *Carnegie Report* was one of several such examinations of professional schools; two of the others were medical schools and seminaries. We think of those as service professions because they are. Practitioners in both fields spend their days tending to the physical and spiritual needs of others. The reports examining those curricula and teaching methods reveal that both are very intentional (and even self-conscious) about

12. Michael Simkovic & Frank McIntyre, *The Economic Value of a Law Degree*, 43 J. Legal Stud. 249, 284 (2014); *See generally*, Michael Simkovic & Frank McIntyre, *The Value of a Law Degree by College Major*, 68 J. Legal Educ. 585 (2019).

connecting their students to a service orientation. In law school we have some clinics that do this, but do we do this anywhere else in legal education, with intentionality, in a way that will impact every student? We do not.[13]

Many law students come to law school with a service orientation in mind.[14] They want to serve the public good—help to address climate change, and broaden equity and diversity in the world around them—for example. But by the time they graduate, this admirable orientation has been much reduced, if not eliminated.[15] This is not just to be written off as maturation about the world—it is a tragedy, and one for which legal education bears some responsibility.

How to Create a Service Orientation Across the Curriculum

In the first year of law school, in the hybrid form proposed in Chapter Six, each of the doctrinal courses can select cases and use hypotheticals that stress the service aspects of the profession. This can be accomplished through examples and selection of cases for students to read and discuss. Group projects should be designed around client-centered problem sets. These sorts of changes are not difficult to make within the confines of the expected "content" of the course, but they do involve some intentional effort and emphasis.

After the hybrid first year, the curriculum opens up with the addition of experiential learning opportunities, including the full-year lawyering course, where students are placed in roles—as attorneys—either in simulation courses or the clinic. There would still be required classes such as Evidence and Legal Ethics, and these could be presented in a hybrid fashion, with some content in an online lecture format and the rest in class discussion or group work. Legal Ethics, of course, inevitably emphasizes the service aspect of what lawyers do, and their ethical obligations. But the experiential opportunities are where

13. As noted in Chapter Three, the faith-based schools are in a better position to do this. The Mission Statement of St. Thomas Law School is: "The University of St. Thomas School of Law, as a Catholic law school, is dedicated to integrating faith and reason in the search for truth through a focus on morality and social justice." *About St. Thomas Law*, Univ. St. Thomas, https://www.stthomas.edu/law/about/ (last visited Aug. 22, 2022).

14. Kennon M. Sheldon & Lawrence S. Krieger, *Does Legal Education Have Undermining Effects on Law Students? Evaluating Changes in Motivation, Values, and Well-Being*, 22 Behav. Scis. & L. 261, 281 (2004).

15. *Id.*

the formation of professional identity should be fostered with intention, and within that, the orientation of service to others.

One law school—at the University of Pittsburgh—appointed a task force in 2013, and it issued a report that recommended the entire curriculum be oriented around the concept of "Preparing for Service."[16] Unfortunately, the long list of recommended changes to the curriculum were not actually oriented around service to others, at least not specifically. It made for a good organizing statement for a collection of changes (such as "expand experiential learning opportunities"), but it did not actually reorient the curriculum around service. Indeed, this statement reveals that it was about competency to practice law: "[Preparing for Service] reflects the proposition that no law school should graduate students into the world of service who are not, in fact, capable of delivering competent services."[17] Pitt Law School's idea of orienting the curriculum around "Preparing for Service" was admirable, but ultimately missed the mark. This is because preparation for service is about more than competency to practice, but rather about much deeper human values.

How to Create a Service Orientation in Each Class

Helping our students to understand that they are preparing to be of service to others can be accomplished in a number of ways. But it starts with faculty, administration. and staff *modeling* the service orientation every day. Because at its best, teaching of all kinds is also a service profession. In his seminal book *The Courage to Teach*, Parker Palmer stresses the importance of establishing a "community of truth" in every classroom to encourage and support deep learning.[18] But he laments that most teaching goes against this principle. Instead, he writes:

> [O]ur conventional pedagogy emerges from a principle that is hardly communal. It centers on a teacher who does little more than deliver conclusions to students. It assumes that the teacher has all the knowledge and the students have little or none, that the teacher sets all the

16. Michael J. Madison, *Preparing for Service: A Template for 21st Century Legal Education* 4–5 (Univ. Pittsburgh Legal Stud. Rsch. Paper No. 2015-17) (available at http //ssrn .com/abstract=2646931).

17. *Id.* at 21.

18. Parker Palmer, The Courage to Teach 54, 116 (Jossey-Bass 1998).

> standards and the students must measure up. Teacher and students gather in the same room at the same time not to experience community but simply to keep the teacher from having to say things more than once.[19]

Establishing a community of truth that models a service orientation in a law school classroom—whether online or hybrid—requires a kind of *love*—specifically, the kind of love described in the ancient Greek concept of *agape*.[20]

To be absolutely clear, when using the word "love," there are those who might recoil, but this would only be through a misunderstanding of the point being made. There are plenty of cases in all levels of education where teachers have abused their position of trust and engaged in a different kind of love—eros. In no way is the use of the word "love" here meant in this way. (Indeed, there probably is no better way than to destroy a community of truth than to engage in an inappropriate relationship with one of your students.) But the ancient Greeks articulated four different kinds of love, including *eros* (the type of love not being suggested here), *storge* (empathy), *philia* (the type of love through which we love our friends and family), and *agape*—which refers to a very different sort of love than the other three. It is also one we do not talk about much, especially in academia.

One of the modern world's most expressive proponent of agape love was Dr. Martin Luther King, who explained through many sermons and writings that agape is not a sentimental or affectionate kind of love, but rather love in the sense of deep understanding and redemptive good will.

> *Agape* means understanding, redeeming good will for all men. It is an overflowing love which is purely spontaneous, unmotivated, groundless, and creative. It is not set in motion by any quality or function of its object.... It is a love in which the individual seeks not his own good, but the good of his neighbor. *Agape* does not begin by discriminating between worthy and unworthy people, or any qualities people possess. It begins by loving others *for their sakes*. It is an entirely "neighbor-regarding concern for others," which discovers the

---

19. *Id.* at 118.

20. Portions of this chapter were previously published in David I. C. Thomson, *What We Do: The Life and Work of the Legal Writing Professor*, 50:2 J. Law & Educ. 171 (2021) and are reprinted here with permission.

> neighbor in every [one] it meets.... Consequently, the best way to assure oneself that love is disinterested is to have love for the enemy-neighbor from whom you can expect no good in return, but only hostility and persecution.[21]

Most faith traditions also contain this concept. The notion of agape is nearly identical to one of Buddhism's four *brahmaviharas*, or divine attitudes—the concept of *Metta*, often translated as universal love.[22] In Japanese culture, it is expressed in the word *amae*, or "indulgent love," that dictates that all relationships should be based on the kind of love that indulges people's needs as well as their idiosyncrasies, even when it is difficult to do so.[23] Christianity also contains the concept and uses it to describe God's love for man. The passage of the Bible often used in wedding ceremonies—from St. Paul's letter to the Corinthians—speaks to this:

> If I speak in the tongues of men and of angels, but have not love, I am a noisy gong or clanging cymbal. And if I have prophetic powers, and understand all mysteries and all knowledge, and if I have all faith, so as to remove mountains, but have not love, I am nothing. Love is patient and kind; love is not jealous or boastful; it is not arrogant or rude. Love does not insist on its own way; it is not irritable or resentful; it does not rejoice at wrong but rejoices in the right. Love bears all things, believes all things, hopes all things, endures all things.[24]

Oxford University Professor C.S. Lewis describes this as a selfless love, a love that is passionately committed to the well-being of another and argues that it is the "greatest of all" the four loves.[25] This kind of love transcends and *serves* regardless of circumstances.

---

21. Martin Luther King, Jr., A Testament of Hope: The Essential Writings and Speeches of Martin Luther King, Jr. 19 (Harper One 1990).

22. *See* Encyclopedia of Buddhism 34 (Damien Keown & Charles S. Prebish, eds., Routledge 3d ed. 2010).

23. Takeo Doi, *Amae no kozo* [The Anatomy of Dependence] (1971); *see also* 'Amae,' Intercultural Word Sensei, https://interculturalwordsensei.org/%E7%94%98%E3%81%88-amae/ (last visited Aug. 22, 2022).

24. King, *supra* note 21, at 20.

25. C.S. Lewis, The Four Loves 4–5 (HarperOne Reissue Ed. 2017).

A related concept of service to others in the Christian tradition is one of the three virtues, *caritas*, or charity. This refers to charity towards others through an altruistic love for them, particularly those less fortunate than ourselves. While that might seem like a stretch in the context of legal education, it is not. We forget sometimes that we are incredibly fortunate and privileged to have been able to go to law school ourselves and excelled enough at it that we became law professors. Many of our students are struggling to get through the day, and they (mostly temporarily) hate us for piling on the work. We might have to do so for pedagogical reasons, but when we lose touch with our student's struggles, we bruise the community of truth we want to establish and maintain in the classroom—students are never our enemies. When, for example, you hear a colleague or two complaining about their students (late to class, surfing on their laptops, etc.) this sets up a dynamic that can damage community. Dr. King reminds us of the centrality of community in the concept of agape this way:

> *Agape* is not a weak, passive love. It is love in action.... *Agape* is a willingness to go to any length to restore community.... It is a willingness to forgive, not seven times, but seventy times seven to restore community.... If I respond to hate with a reciprocal hate I do nothing but intensify the cleavage in broken community. I can only close the gap in broken community by meeting hate with love.[26]

The idea of applying this sort of love to students is not a common one, but it is also not a new one. The progressive eighteenth century Swiss educator Johann Heinrich Pestalozzi was groundbreaking for his work educating the whole student, seeking to achieve "an equilibrium of what he called 'head, hands and heart.'"[27] Pestalozzi believed there was an "inner dignity" to each student, and that "without love, neither the physical nor the intellectual powers will develop naturally."[28]

More recently, at least one law school dean of students has discovered the benefit of selfless love when working with students. In an article by Associate

---

26. King, *supra* note 21, at 20.

27. Annik LaFarge, Chasing Chopin 66 (Simon & Shuster 2020). This sounds a lot like the integrated learning model proposed in the *Carnegie Report*. *See* discussion in Chapter One.

28. *Id.*

Dean David B. Jaffe entitled *The Key to Law Student Well-Being? We Have to Love our Law Students*, he describes the ways in which deans, faculty, and the admissions and orientation processes can all be reoriented to greater care of our students during their time in our law schools. "Together, greater expressions of love to our students and attention to their wellness and mental health can only result in these individuals experiencing more healthy and productive lives in law school and in the profession."[29]

In contrast, too often in legal teaching, we feel like we have to use fear to motivate our students. Fear of the grade, fear of a withheld letter of recommendation, but more immediately—fear of in-class humiliation. The "Socratic Method"—so famous in law school—often involves humiliation of one kind or another. But there are at least two problems with using fear or humiliation as a teaching technique. First, if we ever humiliate or insult a student, the lesson is quite plainly over—not only for that student, but for similarly situated ones as well. It is just not an effective way to open a channel for learning—instead, it shuts it down and creates unnecessary student stress.[30] Second, as Barbara McClintock's work says about the kind of love great teachers have for their students, it is a kind of "intimacy without the annihilation of difference."[31] Through this lens, teaching through humiliation not only shuts down student learning and bruises community, but it also serves to undermine inclusive teaching practices. All of our students, regardless of circumstances, race, gender, sexual orientation, or any other kind of difference from the "mainstream," deserve to be treated with equal dignity, respect, and, yes, love. Of course, when you have a student who is struggling, and you treat them with equal respect and dignity, it is good to remember that everyone else in the class is watching you do that, and you also strengthen the community of trust as a whole.

In looking for ways to start thinking about a new and invigorated orientation around service in your law school, the often-overlooked members of each law school's faculty would be a good place to start. This is because most of them

29. David B. Jafee, *The Key to Law Student Well-Being? We Have to Love our Law Students*, PD Q., Feb. 2018, at 16. If there is a silver lining to the 2020–22 Covid pandemic, it is that it seems to have encouraged all faculty to acknowledge and emphasize the importance of mental health and wellness more than we have in the past.

30. Debra S. Austin, *Positive Legal Education: Flourishing Law Students and Thriving Law Schools*, 77 MD. L. Rev. 649, 649 (2018).

31. Evelyn Fox Keller, A Feeling for the Organism: The Life and Work of Barbara McClintock 200 (Freeman 1983).

already teach in this way. Look to your dean of students, and their staff, who go a long way toward setting a standard around service. You should also consider your bar passage faculty as well as your academic achievement faculty and legal writing faculty, who engage in this sort of teaching every day.[32]

Lack of Faculty Equity Undermines a Service Orientation

In the first year, law students are often unaware of the status divisions typical to most law faculties. They refer to all their teachers as "professor" and do not know that some of them enjoy the benefits of tenure and some do not, that they are paid substantially differently, that some are subject to mistreatment[33] by tenured faculty, and that some have no governance rights on the faculty they have been a faithful member of for decades. But usually by the second and third year, quite a few students learn about these divisions. And it undermines their faith that they are part of an institution that professes non-discrimination and yet behaves differently. That they are part of an institution that believes in fairness, justice, and equality and yet behaves differently. It sends a strong message that undermines any attempt to adopt a service orientation, because it sends the opposite message: that even the people who are entrusted with teaching them and preparing them for a life of service to others are engaged in the same internecine and hierarchical divisions that the school professes are wrong in our society and need to be eradicated. And again, our legitimacy as an institution that upholds the rule of law, that protects our democratic institutions, and that seeks to lift up and empower historically underrepresented groups is jeopardized. To adopt a service orientation in our law schools we must be scrupulously consistent, no matter how hard it might be.

---

32. *See generally* David I. C. Thomson, *What We Do: The Life and Work of the Legal Writing Professor*, 50:2 J. L. & Educ. 703 (2021). *See also*, Linda H. Edwards, The Doctrine-Skills Divide: Legal Education's Self-Inflicted Wound (Carolina Acad. Press 2017).

33. Nantiya Ruan, *Papercuts: Hierarchical Microagressions in Law Schools*, 31 Hastings Women's L.J. 3, 15 (2019).

Conclusion

Law schools deserve some of the blame for the ethical issues facing the profession. But not for the assumed reason: that we do not teach the ethical rules properly or thoroughly. We actually do that fairly well, and our students regularly pass the ethics examination required in all fifty states.

Rather, we deserve some of the blame because we have lost our way in our mission, and thus so has the profession. We have continued to admit already privileged students in large numbers who are seeking law school as a way to stay in the upper middle class of society, and who leave law school barely aware of the ideal of a lawyer with a strong professional identity and moral compass and with an orientation to service.

Many of our graduates leave law school only lightly trained on the lawyer's obligation to uphold the rule of law, advance our democratic institutions, and serve the public good. But they do leave law school burdened by their tremendous debt loads. Only a few are able to join high-paying law firms that impose unreasonably high workloads for compensation that allows them to pay down the debt. Unfortunately, these firms often represent clients at odds with the values of this generation of graduates—ones that prioritize profits over people and press releases over actual change around systemic racism, environmental concerns, and human health. The students who cannot join these firms rely on a precarious system of loan forgiveness for public service jobs, or they spend the next 20 years paying off their loans. Through these routes, and others, many of our graduates feel forced to set aside the service orientation they brought to law school because the system requires it and we have not emphasized it in our teaching or modeled it in our governance of the law school they have paid so much to attend.

EIGHT

The Usual Objections Are Unfounded

Introduction

By this point in the book—if not earlier—many law school faculty members or administrators will likely be concerned about how the model proposed here would play out practically in their law schools, seeing substantial disruption in the details. But this chapter seeks to put those concerns to rest. While the proposals made here involve shifting some resources, they do not require immediate or radical transformation of every current aspect of legal education. We still—very much—need tenured faculty who publish scholarship, for example.

Overnight Change Is Not Necessary

It has been said that the only change that happens in law schools is that which is so slow that no one notices. Whether that is true or not, this book does not—in any way—intend to argue that the changes in law school that it advocates should take place immediately, or all at once, or in every school in the same way. There will be, and should be, a period of experimentation. Some schools will lead the way in this, being committed to doing so, or just needing to for various financial reasons or otherwise. Indeed, some schools have led the way in developing a hybrid part-time law school program, and these are having considerable success.[1] Other schools should look to those schools for models of how to experiment with hybrid legal education before attempting to implement it in their own schools. And when they do, it is much better to start small. It will take at least a decade—and likely more—for the proposals contained in this book to be implemented widely in law schools. Even then, some schools will have little hybrid course work in the first year, and some will build a hybrid online part time program, and eventually find that it takes over parts of the traditional 1L cohort for them. Increasingly, our students are looking for innovative alternatives to giving up their jobs and taking on substantial tuition and living expense debt. As long as they can be assured it is "real" law school, and will give them the same credential, there will be demand for it.

Removing the LSAT Will Not Cause Other Problems

The removal of the LSAT as a criterion for admission can also be accomplished gradually. The ABA has recently proposed lifting the requirement of the LSAT or GRE.[2] Law school admissions offices should be encouraged and allowed latitude to experiment with alternate admissions criteria and to compile data on how those students performed. The Foundations for Practice study provides a guide for alternate criteria that can be used.[3] Deans will probably need to expand their admissions staffing to accomplish this work over a three-to-seven-year period. If the legal academy can develop alternate admissions criteria that are as predictive of performance in law school and bar passage as the LSAT has been (which has a correlation, but a weak one[4]), this is one of the most important things we can do: encourage the admissions office at your school to experiment in the development of alternate admissions criteria.

1. Shuai Wang et al., *An Evaluation of a First-of-its-kind Hybrid Law Degree Program*, 34 J. Comput. Higher Educ. 517, 519–20 (2022).

2. Memorandum from Council to the Strategic Rev. Comm. (April 25, 2022) available at https://www.americanbar.org/content/dam/aba/administrative/legal_education_and_admissions_to_the_bar/council_reports_and_resolutions/may22/22-may-memo-revisions-501-503.pdf.

3. Alli Gerkman & Logan Cornett, *Foundations for Practice: Survey Overview and Methodological Approach*, IAALS, Univ. Denv. (July 26, 2016), https://iaals.du.edu/publications/foundations-practice-survey-overview-and-methodological-approach.

4. *See* Marjorie M. Shultz & Sheldon Zedeck, *Predicting Lawyering Effectiveness: Broadening Law School Admission Decisions*, 36 L. & Soc. Inquiry 620, 621 (2018).

Academic Freedom and Scholarship Remain Imperative

The great concern, as always, is that any form of change will reduce academic freedom and scholarly production. Both are core values for university graduate education and must remain so. But as the hybrid part-time program expands, and faculty are needed to teach in it, this has usually been done voluntarily, or perhaps in exchange for a small financial incentive. And as long as there are financial and other supports for scholarship, there should be no threat there. Encouraging faculty to include a service component in all of their classes may be more difficult, but with sufficient training and help this can be mitigated. And given the nature of the request—to figure out a way to engage students in a service orientation to the work—it should not be resisted broadly or substantively.

Retooling the Faculty May Be Necessary to Some Degree

It is true that some faculty will need additional help and support to convert their teaching model to a hybrid format. Fortunately, all universities—and some law schools as well—now have robust support in place in the form of instructional designers, video technicians, and technology support. Many universities also offer classrooms designed for hybrid instruction and flexible in-person instruction, with movable desks and multiple screens. Again, the growth and success of the hybrid part-time programs at law schools around the country show that these changes are necessary and that they are within the abilities of every willing law professor and can be financially successful.

This Will Boost Law School Rankings

Law school rankings are always a concern when change to the legal education model is being discussed. If the LSAT is dispensed with, then a different criterion will have to be found. But this is already happening with the US News specialty program rankings[5] and the alternative rankings hosted by other

5. Robert R. Kuehn, *Law School Specialty Program Rankings: Is the Tail Wagging the Dog?*, Best Practices blog (May 4, 2019), https://bestpracticeslegaled.com/2019/05/04/law-school-specialty-program-rankings-is-the-tail-wagging-the-dog/

magazines.[6] Also, the US News ranking process now includes total student indebtedness as a negative criterion weighing on each law school's rankings. Schools that are able to reduce that—through a less costly hybrid 1L year, for example—seem poised to substantially rise in the rankings.

Net Tuition Revenue Does Not Change

Law schools adopting a mostly online 1L year for their program of legal education would receive the same tuition revenue that they currently receive because they would admit many more students to that first year—and would be able to admit more diverse applicants—delivering the basic first year instruction at a much lower cost. Students in a larger entering class could then discover and show that they have a facility for learning this material—not on one discriminatory test, but over the course of perhaps even two years while they work at other jobs, which would, of course, also lower the opportunity cost for them.

Understandably, some readers might want budgetary detail supporting this proposal, which ideally should work for different types of schools, levels of enrollment, and net tuition. A close study of the ABA 509 Disclosures[7] for schools selected in six categories reveals that, with slight modifications, this proposal preserves net tuition revenue.

The schools studied were selected in the following categories: public/large (453 students in the 1L class), public/medium (251), public/small (119), private/large (417), private/medium (256), and private/small (115), and were taken from the 2021 ABA 509 Disclosure site,[8] which collects the 509 disclosures submitted by each accredited law school every year. Net tuition revenue was calculated using information available in the 509 disclosures and the formula used for the same purpose by the ABA Task Force on Financing Legal Education.[9]

---

6. Examples of these rankings can be found in preLaw Magazine, published by National Jurist. For more information, *see* https://nationaljurist.com/prelaw/rankings/.

7. The annual ABA 509 Disclosure documents may be reviewed at this web address: https://abarequireddisclosures.org/Disclosure509.aspx.

8. *Id.*

9. *See* Report of the ABA Task Force on Financing Legal Education (A.B.A., June 17, 2015) available at https://www.americanbar.org/content/dam/aba/administrative/legal_education_and_admissions_to_the_bar/reports/2015_june_report_of_the_aba_task_force_on_the_financing_of_legal_education.pdf. The formula for net tuition rates used

Using this data and the formula for net tuition indicate that for each school in each of the six categories, doubling the incoming class for 1L, reducing the tuition for that year to between $10,000 and $15,000, passing between 50 percent and 59 percent of the class on to 2L, and charging the same net tuition for 2L and 3L results in an *increase* in net tuition over the current three-year course of law school in each case. For example, the school selected in the private/small category has an enrollment of 119 students and charges a net tuition of $24,068 per year, for a three-year net tuition budget of $8,592,276. If that school admitted 238 students for the 1L hybrid/online year at a tuition rate of $10,000 ($2,856,000) and passed 55 percent (129 students) to the 2L and 3L year at $24,068 ($3,110,789), that school would net $9,077,576 for the three-year net tuition, providing an increase of $485,300 in net tuition. It should be noted, of course, that there would be ten additional students that pass on to 2L under a 55 percent pass rate, but the increased tuition should provide sufficient additional resources to cover any additional expenses that would entail.

Similarly, the formula works for the law school selected in the public/medium category, which has an enrollment of 265 students and charges a net tuition of $27,239, for a three-year net tuition budget of $21,655,005. If that school admitted 530 students at $13,000 ($6,890,000) and passed 55 percent (291) to the 2L and 3L years at $27,239 ($15,880,337), that school would receive $22,770337 for the three-year net tuition, providing an increase of $1,115,332 in net tuition. Having a larger initial class size of 265, doubling it, and taking 55 percent would result in 26 additional students for 2L and 3L. But again, an increase of $1.15M in net tuition should cover any additional expenses caused by the larger upper-class sizes.

The formula also works for the school selected in the private/large category, although it requires stretching to the upper limit of the formula when the net tuition of that school is higher than most. That school has an enrollment of 453 students and a $45,601 net tuition, for a three-year net tuition budget of $61,971,759. If that school admitted 906 students to the 1L hybrid year it would need to charge $15,000 per year ($13,590,000) and have a pass rate of 59 percent of the class for 2L and 3L years, which would admit 534 to

---

here was the same used in the report: "First, subtract the median award from the sticker price and multiply that figure by the percentage of full-time students receiving free money; second, multiply the sticker price by the percentage of students paying sticker price; and finally, to get a school's overall net price add together the figures from the first two steps." *Id.* at 25.

those classes and net $48,751,117, for a total of $62,341,117 and an increase of $369,358. The additional 81 students in this model is admittedly a lot, and could be mitigated by increasing the 1L tuition, which—compared to $45,601 for this school—would seem in comparison much lower, and thus allowing a reduction in the pass rate, resulting in a smaller 2L and 3L classes.

When the institution has a large student class size but is a public institution—which usually reduces the tuition cost—the pass rate can be reduced. The school selected in the public/large category has an enrollment of 417 students and charges a net tuition of $22,771, for a three-year net tuition budget of $28,486,521. If that school admitted 834 students at $12,000 ($10,056,000) and passed 50 percent (417) to the 2L and 3L years at $22,771 ($18,991,014) that school would net $29,047,014 for the three-year net tuition, providing a net tuition increase of $560,493, with *no* additional students passing on to the 2L and 3L years.

The same formula works for schools selected for the study in the private/medium (251/$33,730) and the public/small categories (115/$14,128). In the former institution if there were a doubling of the 1L class at a rate of $13,000 and pass rate of 56 percent, there would be a net tuition increase (with 30 additional students). And also there is a net tuition benefit for the latter institution, with a 1L tuition rate of just $10,000 and a pass rate of 50 percent for the public/small institution (with no additional students).

LLLTs Will Continue to Expand

As states expand the availability of the Limited License Legal Technician (LLLT) certification, law schools are best positioned to train students for this kind of career. And schools could work with their local bar to make sure that students who will end their law school experience with the hybrid first year will be awarded a master's degree in American Law. If law schools doubled the first year cohort in size and admitted half of that cohort to the primarily in-person second and third year classes, then the other half of each 1L cohort would be awarded the master's degree, and have the opportunity to become an LLLT (with lower debt, so they could afford lower fees for that work). But even if they did not go on to the LLLT career track, it would be a net good of significant proportion to have that many more citizens in this country who understand how the law works, and how important the rule of law is to the functioning of our democracy, which is another way our law schools could live into their responsibility to uphold and defend our democratic institutions.

As options for a second career track short of requiring the J.D. develop, many students will choose to take just the first year of law school, receive the master's degree, and at much lower cost seek out a career as an LLLT. However, many students will want to advance to finish the J.D., and if they do well enough in the intensive examinations (sometimes referred to as a "baby bar") to be admitted, the "second" year would include the full lawyering (Legal Writing) course and the remaining core courses in the first semester (such as Constitutional Law and Administrative Law). Students would then transition to more simulation-based experiential learning in the spring semester, including training in legal research, writing, and advocacy. "Third" year would continue with more experiential learning and add a supervised externship and a clinic. Students taking an externship can now be paid a modest amount for their work,[10] thus reducing the cost of tuition further.[11]

We Might Need to Change Some Classroom Configurations

We will need two changes to the physical plant of most law schools, but again, this can happen over time. We need smaller libraries than we did when many of these school buildings were being built. The reduction in law libraries—and their budgets—is already happening. And we will need fewer large lecture hall classrooms than we did before. Over time, these can be converted to smaller classrooms, with collaborative working spaces. But again, this should not need to be done for some time and can be planned and budgeted well in advance.

Expansion of Experiential Learning Will Not Markedly Increase Expenses

Clinical and externship programs would remain much the same. They are already focused on the practical education that the second and third year currently offer and would continue to offer. There is value in developing

10. Chris Morgan, *A Case for Paid Externships*, A.B.A. L. Students (Nov. 2, 2016), http://abaforlawstudents.com/2016/11/02/the-case-for-paid-law-student-externships.

11. For a more detailed explanation of the 1L curriculum proposed in this book, *see* Chapter Six.

additional whole course simulation courses, which are cheaper than clinics,[12] and uniquely prepare students for the clinical and externship steps that follow. Currently, in many schools, externships use up the available practical education credits, and there are not enough students who still have credits to "spend" on these valuable simulation courses. This can be addressed by expanding those credits, and professors already on the payroll can develop these. Appointing an associate dean of experiential learning, as many schools have done,[13] can help to balance these competing interests and give a voice to that side of the curriculum.

Law School Will Not Become Commodified

One concern that often comes up is that, under this model, law school will just become a "MOOC." Perhaps a reminder of the terms that make up the acronym would be helpful: **Massive** refers to a large number of enrollees. **Open** refers to the fact that these courses are typically offered to anyone in the world. **Online** indicates that they are fully online courses, with no face-to-face contact. **Courses** seems obvious, but is not; since enrollees can come and go, complete as much or as little as they want, and do not necessarily receive a grade or any transferrable credit, it stretches the term.

To be clear, this book does *not* recommend that the first year of law school be turned into a MOOC. This model for education, after much hype ten years ago, has mostly failed. This happened for several reasons: First, because MOOCs were primarily a university marketing scheme on the one hand and a public service on the other. MIT and Stanford and Harvard and UVA (etc.) all want their "brand" to extend as far as possible around the world. Offering a few courses by their best professors is a good way to do that. And our most elite institutions *should* be offering a public service of this kind to the world. But while many students signed up, few completed the courses. Second, because education does not scale to that degree. A teacher cannot teach 100,000 students ever, much less in a semester. Third, education—particularly graduate

---

12. Martin J. Katz, *Understanding the Costs of Experiential Legal Education*, 1 J. Experiential Learning 28, 29, 53–56 (2014). *See also* the discussion of whole-course simulation courses in Chapter Three.

13. Binny Miller, *Cultural Brokers in the Changing Landscape of Legal Education: Associate Deans for Experiential Learning*, 2 J. Experiential Learning 98, 103 (2017).

education—is (for most schools) tied to the local market for its graduates as much, and often more than, the reputation of the school.

So, a successful hybrid first year of law school is still "sited" in the physical law building and its city, even if a lot of the work is completed at distance. It still involves regular interaction with the professor, even if moderated through a teaching assistant on occasion.

The Bar Examination Is Already Changing, and We Will Have to Respond

Whenever change in legal education is discussed, there is always the specter of the bar exam as a limiting factor. It is most certainly important that our graduates are able to pass the bar; otherwise, they have spent a great deal of money and time and are unable to use the degree for the purpose they obtained it. But this proposed model for legal education should have no impact on bar passage, for two reasons. First, the same "bar" content is being taught in the hybrid first year doctrinal courses. Second, some might worry that if we dispense with the LSAT (as this book argues we must), our bar passage numbers will go down. But Professors Scott Johns[14] and Louis Schulze[15] have shown in their research that students with lower LSAT scores can pass the bar with focused support and using teaching techniques such as spaced repetition, concept mapping, and essay feedback. So even if a student, who if they had taken it would have scored below the threshold the school previously used for admission, would be admitted without the LSAT, with focused help and support they can still pass the bar exam.

But most importantly, this book proposes that students must get through a rigorous test at the end of the first year to progress to the second and third year in the program.[16] Somewhat less than half will not pass, although most of

---

14. Scott Johns, *Empirical Reflections: A Statistical Evaluation of Bar Exam Program Interventions*, 54 U. Louisville L. Rev. 35, 68 (2016).

15. Louis N. Schulze, Jr., *Using Science to Build Better Learners: One School's Successful Efforts to Raise Its Bar Passage Rates in an Era of Decline*, 68 J. Legal Educ. 230, 259 (2019).

16. Fortunately, there is already a model for this: the First Year Law Student's Exam, colloquially known as the "Baby Bar" exam in California. But it is not necessary that each school use a state-sponsored test at the end of the first year—that is an artifact of the California law school accreditation process, which other states do not have. Each school could develop its own test for this end of first year exam.

those will receive a master's degree in American Law. Many of those are likely the students who would struggle to pass the bar, so if anything, this proposal should *increase* bar passage rates. Further, it will remove most of those graduates who might take a bar exam and not pass after investing three years and all that money into law school.

Further, it must be noted that the bar exam has its own issues with discriminatory impact and relevance to the practice of law. The California Bar reduced the "cut score" (or passing mark) in that state, perhaps after reflecting on the research indicating that bar exam cut scores have an uneven and discriminatory impact, with little or no improvement in the protection of the public.[17] Further, an empirical analysis of the Uniform Bar Exam, used in thirty-six states, indicates racial bias in the test itself.[18]

Of great interest to law schools should be the effort underway at the National Conference of Bar Examiners (NCBE) to make the bar exam more relevant to the practice of law. The "NextGen" bar exam will be administered to graduates of law schools in 2026, thus applying to those students matriculating in law school in the fall of 2023.[19] The NextGen bar exam, which is gaining momentum around its proposed form, acknowledges that the current exam requires too much memorization, and does not do enough to test legal practice skills. The new exam, to be adopted by some proportion of the thirty-six UBE states, will still rely on the first year courses and will add Evidence and Business Associations.[20] The test will present problems as they might arise in practice, merging several subject areas and including multiple-choice questions, short-answer questions, and essays or practice-oriented documents (such as a legal memo).

17. Michael B. Fisby, Sam C. Erman & Victor D. Quintanilla, *Safeguard or Barrier: An Empirical Examination of Bar Exam Cut Scores*, 70 J. Legal Educ. 125 (2020); Scott Johns, *Putting the Bar Exam on Constitutional Notice: Cut Scores, Race & Ethnicity, and the Public Good*, 45 Seattle U. L. Rev. 1 (2022).

18. Scott Devito, Kelsey Hample & Erin Lain, *Examining the Bar Exam: An Empirical Analysis of Racial Bias in the Uniform Bar Exam*, 55 U. Mich. J.L. Reform 597 (2022).

19. For more information about the plans for the NextGen Bar examination, *see* https://nextgenbarexam.ncbex.org/.

20. The Next Gen Bar will test eight Core Subjects, and seven Foundational Skills. The Core Subjects will be: Civil Procedure, Contracts, Evidence, Torts, Business Associations, Constitutional Law, Criminal Law, and Real Property. *NextGen Bar Exam of the Future, FAQs About Recommendations*, https://nextgenbarexam.ncbex.org/faqs/. The Foundational Skills will be: Legal Research, Legal Writing, Issue Spotting and Analysis, Investigation and Evaluation, Client Counseling and Advising, Negotiation and Dispute Resolution, and Client Relationship and Management. *Id.*

If the bar exam to date has heavily influenced the law school curriculum—and most would agree that it has—then the NextGen bar exam may also influence it in some interesting ways. The design of the new exam suggests that the first year curriculum should break down the silos between subjects it currently has, and that integration of subjects—focused on solving practical problems—would prepare students better for the NextGen bar exam that they will be facing.

The proposals in this book support a similar curricular shift: toward breaking down silos between subjects and greater focus on practice-oriented teaching and learning. One of the great values of moving towards a hybrid online first year of law school is that these sorts of innovations can be integrated more easily through the use of technology, with backward course design focused on achieving measurable learning outcomes. As the national bar exam evolves toward a more practice-oriented model, these lessons can also be applied to the first year "baby bar" exam proposed here.

Conclusion

Law faculties are famously resistant to change, and thus many would believe that it is impossible to get any of the changes proposed in this book approved. Martha Minnow, Dean of Harvard Law School, once famously noted that whenever a new proposal was made to the Harvard law faculty, there would always be this divided argument: "We've never done that before," on one side, and "We've already done that" on the other.[21] As a result of this mindset, no change of substance could get approved.

But the usual objections to the proposals in this book have been dispelled in this chapter. It will have no impact on academic freedom or scholarly output. It may require some retooling by some members of the faculty, but it will be minor because much of that was already accomplished in the pandemic. Reducing student debt will help with law school rankings. Net tuition revenue will not change significantly and may even be increased under this proposal. LLLTs are expanding and law schools have an opportunity to meet that market with new revenue-generating courses and certifications. We may need to redesign some of our classrooms, but that should not be too expensive, and can take place over time. The proposals in this book will not result in the commodifica-

21. Plenary Session, American Association of Law Schools Annual Meeting, *Rethinking Legal Education for the 21st Century*, Jan. 4, 2008.

tion of law schools because it will not supplant place-based instruction. Finally, the bar examination is already changing towards this model.

We are either serious about addressing systemic racism, or we are not. We are either concerned about the law school's role in upholding the rule of law and our democratic institutions, or we are not. We are either in the business of churning out ethically borderline graduates and sending them to the ramparts of protecting the institutions of white privilege, or we are not. The time to stand by and suggest incremental changes is over. The legitimacy of the entire legal education enterprise is in doubt, and systemic change is needed. But there is time, because it need not happen all at once, or in the same way at every law school, or on the same timetable everywhere.

NINE

Conclusion

In her work *Teaching Law: Justice, Politics, and the Demands of Professionalism*, Georgetown Law professor Robin West says this: "We have not developed in the academy an understanding of what the ideal lawyer should know or be trained to do."[1] Professor West's statement is unfortunately true, and damning. This book argues that the reason it is true is because we have lost our way. We are enabling our students to look at the world in an amoral way, relying on the malleability of law to support any legal position. Orienting the law school curriculum around service to others, and—as Professor West argues—a sense of justice (which is also a form of a service orientation), would go a long way to improving legal education, as well as (over time) the profession, and have the important added benefit of strengthening our democratic institutions. And, not least, it would help us keep a better focus on the responsibility to democratize legal education so that our physical and virtual doors are more open to those who traditionally have been excluded.

In his book *Aspiration and Reality in Legal Education*, David Sandomierski describes the study he conducted of contracts professors in Canadian law schools and concludes that what the professors *think* they are teaching significantly diverges from what they are *actually* teaching.[2] And, further, there are structural limitations in legal education to closing that gap, as new professors

1. Robin L. West, Teaching Law: Justice, Politics, and the Demands of Professionalism 151 (Cambridge 2013).

2. David Sandomierski, Aspiration and Reality in Legal Education 339 (Univ. of Toronto Press 2020).

feel they need to conform to what has been done before them.[3] He concludes his book as follows:

> By elucidating the full slate of human qualities that are properly considered the domain of the thinking lawyer, legal educators would strengthen their claim to making a distinctive contribution to the legal profession and to society at large. Although this aspiration remains, for now, unrealized, the requisite theoretical and pedagogical resources are already within contemplation. They just need to be put into practice.[4]

Only a bold path forward will break through these disconnects. With what we have learned in the pandemic about using pedagogical resources to teach in a hybrid way these are no longer within *contemplation*, they are available and in practice. By reengineering the first year of law school and making it more accessible in a hybrid online format, we would remove a significant barrier to entry, lower the cost, and graduate a more diverse class. We could take on teaching more of those "human qualities" to reach the aspirational aspects of "thinking like a lawyer" that Professor Sandomierski elucidates in his study. Further, under the proposals made in this book, those who only take the first year will have much less invested and thus be more able to afford to serve the under-lawyered in our society with a limited license to practice. If we can make these changes, we would go a long way toward addressing the problems that have plagued legal education for decades.

We are often distracted by the latest shiny "total change" toy, and it can take our attention away from critical issues in legal education. Laptops, MOOCs, artificial intelligence—the list goes on. We examine the latest thing, briefly, for fear it may change everything and when satisfied that it will not, we move on. It is irresponsible future-gazing at the expense of the hard work we should be doing now. And it is easier—and lazier—than engaging with hard changes that need to be begun, some of them urgently.

The default teaching mode for the last four centuries was for professors to be the learned scholars behind the podium, what is sometimes called the "Sage on the Stage." But this model of teaching does not work as well with this generation of students. The modern student has so many different distractions, is digitally soaked and marinated, and often has trouble sitting still for the

---

3. *Id.* at 310.

4. *Id.* at 340.

length of our typical classes. Online pedagogy actually helps with this, because it demands careful course design and "chunking" of content into smaller more digestible components. By learning through formative assessment activities, students keep moving, see progress, and stay more engaged.

We should be deeply concerned by the growing evidence that the way we are currently teaching our students actively harms them.[5] What possible justification could there be for doing that?

Instead of thinking of ourselves as the "Sage on the Stage" we should think of ourselves as the "Guide on the Side."[6] Where instead of thinking of our students as vessels for *our* knowledge, we think of them as co-creators of *their* knowledge with our assistance and guidance. Online learning environments help us do this, in a way that is hard to replicate in the traditional classroom. Thus, teaching in a hybrid online environment—particularly one that has been well designed from back to front (and usually with the help of an instructional designer)—will lead to improvements in learning, and provide teaching that is centered around students and help them prepare for their role of service to others.

Another advantage of this model is that it justifies and uses the third year more effectively, thus responding to the critics who would have us dispense with the third year of law school. Because it opens the first year to a larger cohort of students, it protects, and potentially expands, revenue from the first year class.

The changes to legal education proposed in this book seem daunting and difficult. But they are neither. Indeed, gradual movement down this path is already strong—we just may not have noticed it yet. The question of "when?" is a common one but cannot be fixed to a date or exact timeframe and will be different for each school—indeed it may minimally touch some and maximally touch others. But the overall evidence is strong that many of these changes are as inevitable as the weather. The signs are all around.

---

5. Kennon M. Sheldon & Lawrence S. Krieger, *Does Legal Education Have Undermining Effects on Law Students? Evaluating Changes in Motivation, Values, and Well-Being*, 22 Behav. Scis. & L. 261, 281 (2004); Debra S. Austin, *Killing Them Softly: Neuroscience Reveals How Brain Cells Die from Law School Stress and How Neural Self-Hacking Can Optimize Cognitive Performance*, 59 Loy. L. Rev. 791, 793–797 (2013); Carrie Yang Costello, Professional Identity Crisis: Race, Class, Gender, and Success at Professional Schools 82 (Vanderbilt Univ. Press 2005).

6. David I. C. Thomson, *Sometimes You Have to Be The Guide On The Side*, 20 Second Draft 23 (2005).

Many law schools already have an online, part-time program in place, and early evidence indicates that students want more flexibility in their learning modalities even in the full-time program. Our students are living hybrid lives and will continue to do so. The ABA has already proposed dispensing with the LSAT. California has experience with a bar exam after the first year, and it works. Limited License programs are growing in several states, and more are considering them. Bar examiners are moving towards a more equitable approach to their work, and the three-year bar exam instrument is already undergoing a significant shift toward practical legal skills. Many law schools also have experience granting master's degrees, and the proposal to provide an M.A. to a one-year program and a J.D. to a longer program of study has a long tradition in the academy with the M.A. as a precursor to the Ph.D. The medical profession has already shown us the way toward a bifurcated profession, with the advent of nurse practitioners, physician's assistants, and a plethora of other health professionals who provide the necessary services at lower cost.

An interesting question—beyond the scope of this book—is what changes to legal education might also take place in law schools of other countries in the near future. After all, education in those countries *also* had to adjust abruptly during the pandemic, and *also* learned a lot about the efficacy of online learning in the process. In the introductory chapter to their book of essays *The Globalization of Legal Education*, Bryant Garth and Gregory Shaffer explain that many democratic countries around the world designed their legal education systems around the model prevalent in the United States,[7] and how that design attained "particular influence" around the world.[8] And further, that "there is even greater local demand for legal education reform modeled after the United States."[9] Thus it follows that the problems in legal education described in this book also beset legal education in other countries.[10] Some of those programs are in undergraduate degree form, and others in master's degree form, but many countries are moving towards a doctoral degree format, just as we have in the United States. Further, universities in those countries are also trying to open their law curricula to innovations of the last thirty years in the United States, such as developing (or expanding) "practical" edu-

7. Bryant Garth & Gregory Shaffer, eds., The Globalization of Legal Education: A Critical Perspective 14 (Oxford 2022).

8. *Id.* at 28.

9. *Id.* at 14.

10. *See, e.g.*, Sandomierski, *supra* note 2 (describing legal education in Canada).

cation.[11] In some countries—such as Japan—getting into law school is very difficult, and the bar pass mark is set very high.[12] So, while it is beyond the scope of this book, it follows that to the extent to which other countries that originally modeled their legal education systems after the United States have interest in opening up their entry ranks to law school and want to hybridize and integrate their courses and even add professional identity formation and practice-focused courses, the proposals in this book may also be helpful to the legal education programs in those countries.

Whether in the United States or any other country, the changes contemplated here do not have to happen wholesale or be accomplished overnight. But creating a small, part-time hybrid online program has already been accomplished by many law schools without much disruption. Adjusting admissions policies on an experimental basis is not difficult to do and collecting data on student outcomes in these experiments is a relatively simple matter. Exploring and supporting local bar efforts to allow for LLLTs in limited practice areas is something every law school can do. There is no better place than a law school for a specialization program (such as in family law) to be delivered over an additional semester to complete the qualifications for an LLLT position in that field. The evidence becomes overwhelming to at least wonder: "Why *not* try these proposals, on a small scale at first?"

Making these adjustments is a matter of will, and only require that we have a true commitment to do what we can to address the systemic racism in our society (and mitigate legal education's role in it), an increased commitment to defend the democratic institutions our society depends on, and a genuine desire to prepare lawyers for service to others. These are values not unfamiliar to law schools. They have been upheld—in words—forever. We just need to take bold action on those values and embark on a new path forward.

---

11. Maria Voskobitova, Olga Shepeleva & Arkady Gutnikov, *Legal Education in Russia: Historical Overview and Current Reforms*, in Legal Education in Asia 151–52 (Shuvro Prosun Sarker, ed., Eleven Int'l Publ'g, 2014).

12. Noriyuki Asano, *Development and Problems of the New Law School System in Japan*, in Legal Education in Asia, *supra* note 11, at 2.

EPILOGUE

The Students of Today and Tomorrow

It is entirely appropriate that this book ends where it should: with a focus on students.

In the first chapter of *Law School 2.0*, published in 2009, we learned about two fictional law students, Steven Miller and Sasha Lujan, who were offered to illustrate and illuminate themes in the book. Steven was the typical law student of the day, and Sasha the student of the future envisioned by the book.[1]

Sasha had a law school experience that the book envisioned, but that did not quite come to pass (although we are getting closer). It mixed online and in-person learning, hybrid electronic textbooks, and multiple opportunities for experiential learning. But the law school of the future envisioned in that book served her well, and she became an assistant district attorney in her home state of New Mexico. She is now running for Congress.

Meet Jerrold and Irene

In the same spirit, this book introduces two new fictional law students, Jerrold Washington and Irene Begay. Both illustrations are based on stories I have heard from students of color over my quarter century teaching in a law school. I recognize these are not my stories (and they do not apply to all students of color), but they are offered for illustration, with respect and empathy for what some of our students have gone through to attend law school recently, and

1. David I. C. Thomson, Law School 2.0: Legal Education for a Digital Age 1–9 (LexisNexis 2009).

how it might be improved if the proposals in this book were adopted. Jerrold is attending law school now, and Irene is attending law school in the future envisioned by this book.

Jerrold, a Law Student in the Present

Jerrold is from Philadelphia and had no lawyers in his family. But a high school teacher took an interest in him and saw his potential. He helped him apply to, and he was accepted with a scholarship to attend, Temple University. He was a member of Alpha Phi Alpha, where he rose to Chapter President. He was galvanized by the Black Lives Matter protests and decided to attend law school to make a difference in his community. He took the LSAT and achieved a decent score, then took it again to try to improve, and received the same score. He attended a midwestern university law school that offered him a full scholarship. Without a stipend for living expenses, though, he had to take out loans and find a place to live. He found himself one of the few African American students at the law school and looked around his classes and saw few people who looked like him. He did join the Black Law Student Alliance and found friends there. In his first year classes, he often felt that his professors were talking down to him in subtle ways, and assuming that he did not know as much as his white classmates. When he was in college, he found classes fun and engaging (for the most part), but there was low effort at student engagement in his law school classes, and he found them less enjoyable than college was. He experienced various micro-aggressions every day around the law school, but he tried to ignore them. Gradually, they added up, and he started to avoid going to the law school except for class and meetings.

In March of his first year, the pandemic hit, and his professors pivoted their classes online. These were even less engaging than before, but he found he was more comfortable online. The Zoom screens allowed him to be equal to his classmates, and he felt the micro-aggressions were reduced, or at least he felt insulated from them. Second year was a mix of in-person and online, and he liked the flexibility of that, even though the back and forth was disruptive. When he could obtain tapes of classes, he listened to them at double-speed. As a result of this, and not being in the law school building as much, he was able to take on a part-time job, which helped with his living expenses.

In his third year, he took a semester in practice with a big firm downtown, but he sometimes felt out of place and the firm did little to mitigate that. He did like the research projects he was given, and he also did not have to be there all the time, so he could just communicate with the attorney giving him the work. He also did not have to be in the law school building much at all, and he liked that. By spring semester, he had two required courses to finish up, and one of those was fully online, and the other was hybrid. His seminar was with a professor he liked very much, who always welcomed his contributions to the class discussion. He wrote a directed research paper for another professor who was an expert in civil rights law. On graduation he has a job at a civil rights law firm back in Philadelphia. He is worried about passing the bar and is out of money for the expensive bar prep fees—so he will be doing that on his own. Fortunately, his school is offering a bar prep class in the spring semester, and that one is also hybrid. He hopes this will be sufficient, and wishes his school offered more help.

Irene, a Law Student in the Future

Irene, like Sasha, is from New Mexico. She met Sasha at a political fund-raising event and told her she had thought about going to law school, but did not see how it was possible, as she had to stay home to take care of her ailing mother. Sasha explained that her law school had a new program where the first year was mostly online, and much cheaper as a result. If that went well, she could then attend a hybrid version of the second and third years and conduct her externship requirement back in New Mexico. Irene confessed that she was not good at standardized multiple-choice tests, but Sasha explained that law schools do not require the LSAT anymore. So, she applied and went through a rigorous interview schedule, with alumni interviewers local to her. She was accepted. She received a grant from the state for the much reduced first year tuition.

Irene found the online courses interesting and well-designed. She listened to the few lectures, but also watched simulations of the legal concepts, had small-group discussions with her classmates online, and regularly visited online office hours with the professor or the TAs. There were multiple opportunities for feedback—mostly from the TAs—so she was able to make adjustments in her learning of the course material before the final exams. Her many classmates were diverse in age and background and located around the country. She did very well in her first year courses but was wondering how she would be able to go into the hybrid second- and third-year programs at her law school. She also did not know how she would pay for those more expensive years. She had no resources for the rest and was uncertain about taking on any debt. She planned to accept the master's degree in American Law (given to all first year online students who pass) and considered using that to become a LLLT in her state to help people in her community with family law issues. But she applied for financial aid, and because she had done so well in the first year, she received most of her tuition in a scholarship. Because her second year was hybrid, she did not have very high living expenses since she was not at her law school that often, and she slept on a classmate's couch when she needed to be at the law school. In her third year, she obtained a semester in practice posting near her home, so for that semester, she had no additional living expenses.

Irene will graduate having not visited the law school building often, but she will be sure to be there on graduation day. She has a job lined up with the in-house legal office for her tribe, where she will be working on a mix of tribal business issues. She is not too worried about the bar exam because rather than an exercise in memorization, it is now more subject-integrated and skills-based, and she did well in the experiential courses she took in law school and received high marks from her semester in practice job.

Index